T0381466

THE
PURPOSE-DRIVEN
GOD

CRITICAL ISSUES THAT UNDERLIE
GOD'S PASSION FOR THE
COMPLETION OF HIS
GLOBAL MISSION

DENNIS D. COCHRANE

WESTBOW
PRESS°
A DIVISION OF THOMAS NELSON
& ZONDERVAN

This book is a work of non-fiction. Unless otherwise noted, the author and the publisher make no explicit guarantees as to the accuracy of the information contained in this book and in some cases, names of people and places have been altered to protect their privacy.

WestBow Press books may be ordered through booksellers or by contacting:

WestBow Press
A Division of Thomas Nelson & Zondervan
1663 Liberty Drive
Bloomington, IN 47403
www.westbowpress.com
844-714-3454

ISBN: 979-8-3850-3935-7 (sc)
ISBN: 979-8-3850-3936-4 (e)

Library of Congress Control Number: 2024925723

Print information available on the last page.

WestBow Press rev. date: 02/24/2025

CONTENTS

Preface ix

Chapter 1   God–Human Intimacy..............................1
Chapter 2   Universal Worship.................................23
Chapter 3   A Solemn Oath....................................50
Chapter 4   Christ's Inheritance..............................66
Chapter 5   Compassion of God..............................85

Notes 107
Bibliography..119
Epilogue..123
About the Author..125

In grateful acknowledgment of their significant
contributions to the content of this book:

Theron R. Young
Adam A. Hoffman
W. Lindsay Hislop
Paul R. Cochrane

PREFACE

The title of this book might raise eyebrows. "How can Almighty God be driven by anything?" we might ask. Indeed, it would be wrong to suggest that God can be driven by any force external to himself. But God is, in fact, compelled by his own character to do certain things, including the completion of the global mission to which he is irrevocably committed, a mission to bring to himself people from every tribe, language, and nation on earth.

Christ in his earthly ministry was purpose driven. He had a mission to complete, a mission that compelled him to be "obedient to the point of death, even death on a cross."[1] Various translations of Luke 12:50 reveal Christ's all-consuming commitment to the completion of that mission: "I have a baptism to undergo, and how distressed I am until it is completed!"[2] "How distressed I am until it is accomplished!"[3] "I am under a heavy burden until it is accomplished."[4]

This book is an attempt to answer the question, "How important to God is his global mission, and why is the completion of that mission so important to him?" The answer to that question is of the essence, because that mission will be important to us, his human lovers, only as we are aware of its importance to him.

It is no overstatement to say that God is passionate about the completion of his global mission. Passionate? Yes. He is, in fact, a God of passion. The Bible says he hates sin and loves sinners, and he is moved with compassion toward needy people like widows and orphans. He can be grieved but can rejoice with joy comparable to that of a bridegroom rejoicing over his bride.[5]

Without doubt, the God of the Bible is a God of passion, including a passion for the completion of his global mission. But we can know the *intensity* of that passion only as we are aware of the *why* of that passion. This book is about the *why* of that passion.

I heard the late Dr. G. Allen Fleece say, "Missions cannot feed on missions." He went on to explain that without an understanding of what prompts God's missionary passion, it is unlikely that we will embrace the costs of bringing that mission to completion.

The costs can be high. Some parents may need to consent to their children going to a distant part of the world, possibly living in harm's way for the sake of making the Gospel known where it is unknown. Others may need to give up the comfort of living among people of their own language and culture for the sake of completing this mission of God. Some grandparents may need to consent to their grandchildren being taken to a distant part of the world, robbing those grandparents of the joy of watching their grandchildren grow up. Others may need to live what the late Dr. Ralph Winter called a "wartime lifestyle," for the sake of freeing up funds that can help send others to mission frontiers of the world.

Sacrifices of this magnitude require two things: first, a passionate love for God; second, a solid biblical understanding of why the completion of God's global mission is of supreme importance to him. But in seeking such understanding we are confronted by these Bible truths:

> My thoughts are not your thoughts, neither are your ways my ways, declares the LORD. For as the heavens are higher than the earth, so are my ways higher than your ways and my thoughts than your thoughts.[6]
>
> Who has known the mind of the Lord?[7] How unsearchable are his judgments and how inscrutable his ways![8]

But although the thoughts and ways of God are humanly imponderable, we have this God-given assurance: "Call to me and I will answer you and tell you great and unsearchable things you do not know."[9]

That assurance is the hope with which this book is written.

A compilation of Amy Carmichael's devotional thoughts is aptly titled *Edges of His Ways*. That title came from Job's acknowledgment that even his most inspired insights reflected nothing more than the mere fringes of the ways of God.[10] What was true of Job is true of us as well. But how transformative it is to gain even small glimpses of what this global mission of God means to him! Those glimpses can prompt us to join him in the accomplishment of mission objectives that are of enormous importance to him.

It is my prayer that some who read this book will be ruined! Ruined for anything less than wholehearted involvement with God in bringing his mission to completion. Globally. And at whatever cost.

CHAPTER 1

GOD-HUMAN INTIMACY

I t is hard to believe, but the evidence is indisputable: the creator of the vast universe wanted perfect oneness with his human creation—and he paid with his life to achieve it. Nor will he be content until, at last, people from every ethnic nation on earth are forever bonded to him. Completion of his global mission is, therefore, of utmost importance to him.

The opening chapters of the Bible tell of an intimate God–human relationship that once existed. Consider his visits with Adam and Eve: "And they [Adam and Eve] heard the sound of the LORD God walking in the garden in the cool of the day, and the man and his wife hid themselves from the presence of the LORD God among the trees of the garden."[1] This brief text contains radical truth. It reveals the following:

- God came often to that garden. Even before Adam and Eve saw the Lord, they instantly recognized the unique sound of his walking, different from the sound of a walking animal. Their familiarity

1

with that sound tells us they had heard it often, perhaps daily.

- God took physical form. Scripture tells us God is not a physical being.[2] But Adam and Eve heard the sound of physical walking. There is wide agreement among Bible scholars that God took a physical body when he came for those visits with Adam and Eve.

- God laid aside the visible brightness of his glory. Scripture says God "lives in unapproachable light, whom no one has seen or can see."[3] No human eye has ever seen the full brightness of God's glory. Moses was told he would die if he saw that brightness.[4] When Saul of Tarsus saw a light from heaven brighter than the midday Syrian sun, he fell to the ground, blinded by that light. From heaven, he heard a voice saying, "I am Jesus whom you are persecuting."[5] But he later wrote to Timothy, saying that no one—himself included—has ever seen the unapproachable light in which God dwells.[6] Thus, we know that God laid aside his visible brightness for the sake of those visits with Adam and Eve.

- God wanted face time with Adam and Eve. They knew the purpose of his visit, but because of their guilt, they hid from his presence. They didn't want fellowship with him now.

In summary, to spend time with Adam and Eve, God came to that garden often, likely in the person of the preincarnate Christ, to enable fellowship between himself and his human creation.

It isn't possible to overstate God's desire for an intimate relationship with humankind. The depth of his desire is revealed even more fully by his deep grieving when sin entered the picture and deprived him of that cherished relationship. Scripture records his grieving: "The LORD saw that the wickedness of man was great in the earth, and that every intention of the thoughts of his heart was only evil continually ... and it grieved him to his heart."[7]

Some English translations render this text as saying God was grieved "in his heart" or "at his heart." But the literal Hebrew text says he was grieved "to" his heart. There is a significant difference between the prepositions "in" and "to." The former speaks of location, and the latter speaks of distance. How deep was God's grief? He grieved all the way to the core of his being—his heart. One translation attempts to capture the meaning by rendering it as "It broke his heart."[8]

Moses enjoyed a uniquely privileged relationship to the Lord. When Jesus was visibly glorified before three of his disciples, Moses and Elijah were in conversation with him.[9] That special relationship was further seen in the face-to-face relationship Moses enjoyed with the Lord: "The Lord would speak to Moses face to face, as a man speaks with his friend."[10] On two other occasions, scripture refers to this unique face-to-face relationship that existed between the Lord and Moses.[11]

Interpersonal facial relationships are important. It is human instinct to communicate with a person's face. In fact, it is a cause for concern when a listener refuses to give eye contact to the one speaking to him or her.

But Moses's relationship with God was even more poignantly described as a "mouth to mouth" relationship.[12]

Elsewhere, scripture adds to our understanding of the interfacial relationship God seeks with humankind: "The eyes of the LORD are on the righteous, and his ears are attentive to their cry."[13]

Mouth, face, eyes, and ears. God chose anthropomorphic language to reveal the intensity of his desire for two-way interaction with humankind.

My personal experience tells me it is possible to have daily devotional times with the Lord—reading scripture and presenting prayer requests—yet without engaging in loving, two-way, face-to-face interaction with Christ himself. Jesus warned against searching the scriptures without truly encountering him: "You diligently study the Scriptures because you think that by them you possess eternal life. These are the Scriptures that testify about me, yet you refuse to come to me to have life."[14]

It is possible to be drawn to truth—even biblical truth—without being drawn personally to him who said, "I am the way and the truth and the life."[15]

The mission of God is about bringing people into a face-to-face love relationship with him.

The "Whole World" Factor

God was reconciling the world to himself in Christ ...[16] God so loved the world that he gave his one and only Son ...[17] God

did not send his Son into the world to
condemn the world, but to save the world
through him.[18]

From beginning to end, the Bible reveals God's desire
for an intimate relationship with every ethnic part of his
human creation. We will trace that theme throughout
scripture.

Scripture provides abundant evidence of the global
nature of God's mission. Five times in Genesis, we read
of God's promise to bless all nations of the world.

Speaking to Abraham, God said, "All peoples on earth
will be blessed through you."[19] And again, "I will surely
bless you [Abraham] ... and through your offspring all
nations on earth will be blessed."[20] And again, "Through
your offspring [Abraham], all nations on earth will be
blessed."[21]

Speaking about Abraham, God said, "Abraham will
surely become a great and powerful nation, and all nations
on earth will be blessed through him."[22]

God repeated that promise to Isaac: "Through your
offspring all nations on earth will be blessed."[23]

In further affirmation of that promise, God repeated
it yet again to Jacob: "All peoples on earth will be blessed
through you and your offspring."[24]

This promised blessing for all people-nations is not
generic in nature. It is very specific. It is the unique
blessing that would come through that one particular
descendant of Abraham, Christ: "The promises were
spoken to Abraham and to his seed. The Scripture does

not say 'and to seeds,' meaning many people, but 'and to your seed,' meaning one person, who is Christ."[25]

It's a promise of global blessing that would come through Christ—the blessing of salvation.

And what is our part? The psalmist gave us a hint when he prayed, "May God be gracious to us and bless us and make his face shine upon us, that your ways may be known on earth, your salvation among all nations ... all the peoples ... all the ends of the earth."[26]

"Salvation among all nations." That is a primary objective of the mission of God. The importance of that mission cannot be overstated. It is a mission that will be completed at last when people from every ethnic nation are brought into an intimate relationship with God.

I heard the late Don Richardson say, "God never gives dead-end blessing. We are blessed to be a blessing." It was true for Abraham, and it is true for us. God's blessing in our lives is intended ultimately to have a global reach.

It was my privilege to sit briefly under the ministry of the late L. E. Maxwell, founder of Prairie Bible Institute. He noted that too many Christians suffer from "ingrown eyeballs." These are people who pray, "God bless us," without ever adding, "that your ways may be known on earth, your salvation among all nations."

May the Lord save us from ingrown eyeballs!

Christ's parting words to his disciples were not a command. They were a statement of fact: "You will be my witnesses in Jerusalem, and in all Judea and Samaria, and to the ends of the earth."[27]

Years ago, when Bill Clinton was campaigning for

the United States presidency, his chief advisor brilliantly posted these signs on the walls of campaign offices: "It's about the economy, stupid!" In other words, keep the main thing the main thing!

If the global mission of God is of enormous importance to him, why is there in Old Testament scriptures nothing comparable to Christ's command to his disciples to "go and make disciples of all nations"?[28]

The answer to that question can be summed up with two key words: *centrifugal* and *centripetal*. A centrifugal force drives objects away from a center. A centripetal force attracts objects toward a center. In Old Testament times, God's global mission was strategically centripetal in nature. God purposed that Israel should be such a monumental display of his glory that people would come from other nations, seeking to know about Israel's God. To some extent, that did happen, especially during the early years of King Solomon's reign in Israel. Scripture says, "King Solomon was greater in riches and wisdom than all the other kings of the earth. The whole world sought audience with Solomon to hear the wisdom God had put in his heart."[29]

We might say that Solomon held wisdom seminars, with world leaders sitting at his feet and listening to his God-given wisdom. The book of Proverbs may have been a syllabus for those wisdom seminars, seminars in which Solomon wasted no time saying to those world rulers, "The fear of the Lord is the beginning of knowledge … the beginning of wisdom."[30]

But Israel eventually became a dishonor to the Lord, and the mission of God became strategically centrifugal, with Christ saying to his followers, "Go into all the world and proclaim the gospel to the whole creation."[31] In other words, don't wait for people to come to Jerusalem to hear the good news of God.

The Genesis creation story gives us our first clue in understanding why God's mission is global in nature. It reveals the importance he attaches to each particular kind of living being—whether they dwell in water, in air, or on land. Seven times in that creation story, God commanded each of these living beings to multiply "according to their various kinds," or "according to its kind" or "according to their kinds."[32]

Thus, we learn that every kind of God's creation was important to him. Later in scripture, we discover that he wants people of every kind to populate heaven—people from every ethnic nation.

Also noteworthy is the fact that God did not want a sparsely populated planet. He wanted the earth to be filled with his created beings.[33] It shouldn't surprise us, therefore, to learn that he who wanted earth to be filled with every kind of his created life also wants heaven to be filled—filled with an uncountable multitude of people of every kind.[34]

Only when heaven is at last filled with people of every kind will the mission of God be completed. It will be completed not by angels or some other heavenly beings but by followers of Jesus. How noteworthy it is that Christ has given his followers such a critical role in bringing his global mission to completion!

The Wedding Factor

All of heaven awaits a wedding—a climactic event in which Christ, Creator of the universe, will take to himself a human bride. God is passionate about his global mission because, among other things, it has to do with the wedding of His Son.

My wife and I lived for a number of years among the Duna people of Papua New Guinea, none of whom had ever heard of Christ. We had the joy of translating the first portions of Scripture into their language. One morning, as I was having my devotional time with the Lord, I came in my Bible reading to this text:

> Then I heard what sounded like a great multitude, like the roar of rushing waters and like loud peals of thunder, shouting: "Hallelujah! For our Lord God Almighty reigns. Let us rejoice and be glad and give him glory! For the wedding of the Lamb has come, and his bride has made herself ready."[35]

I noticed that the wedding will take place only when Christ's bride has made herself ready. It is especially significant that her readiness is not something done to her or for her. It's something done by her.

I wondered what the bride must do to make herself ready for that wedding. Might it somehow relate to her completion of the task her bridegroom had given her, "Go … and make disciples of all the nations"? This much we know from scripture: Jesus paid a bride price sufficient for a global bride. "He is the atoning sacrifice for our sins, and not only for ours but also for the sins of the whole world."[36]

From scripture, we know Jesus will get what he paid for—a global bride! It is one of the issues that drives the missionary passion of God.

It was an eye-opening experience for me to realize that by making disciples among the Duna people, I was having a part in preparing Christ's bride for that wedding day. I prayed, "Lord, if I never have the privilege of doing anything more than shining the bride's shoes in preparation for that wedding, then I want to spend the rest of my life shining those shoes with everything I've got." And I've been one of the bride's shoeshine boys ever since.

The prophet Zephaniah foresaw a day when the Lord would sing for joy over a redeemed Israel: "The LORD your God is with you .... He will take great delight in you ... will rejoice over you with singing."[37]

Isaiah wrote of that joy saying, "As a bridegroom rejoices over his bride, so will your God rejoice over you."[38]

But there will be another day when heaven will resound with singing. We know the words of that heavenly song: "They sang a new song: You are worthy ... because you were slain and with your blood you purchased men for God from every tribe and language and people and nation."[39]

Imagine what Christ's bride will mean to him—this bride for whom he paid the ultimate bride price, his blood. And consider yourself enormously blessed to have a part in preparing his bride for that day when Christ and his human lovers will be united in a bride-bridegroom relationship.

The Friendship Factor

Can you believe it? God delights in human friends! "[Abraham] was called God's friend."[40] In fact, God himself called Abraham "my friend."[41]

As previously noted, Moses was another friend of God: "The LORD would speak to Moses face to face, as a man speaks with his friend."[42]

But Miriam and Aaron were not impressed. They said, "Has the LORD spoken only through Moses? Hasn't he also spoken through us?"[43]

God's response to Miriam and Aaron reveals how much he treasured his friendship with Moses. God told Miriam and Aaron to come with Moses and stand before him at the door of the tent of meeting. Upon their arrival, he said to Miriam and Aaron, "Listen to my words: When a prophet of the LORD is among you, I reveal myself to him in visions, I speak to him in dreams. But this is not true of my servant Moses; he is faithful in all my house. With him I speak face to face .... Why then were you not afraid to speak against my servant Moses?"[44]

God then struck Miriam with leprosy, healing her only after Moses prayed for her. We do well to notice that it is a serious matter to oppose a friend of God!

Jesus said to his disciples, "I no longer call you servants.... I have called you friends."[45] "I tell you, my friends, do not be afraid of those who kill the body and after that can do no more."[46]

How important to God are human friends? The Bible answers the question. When the entire human race was alienated from him, God sacrificed his Son to again make possible such God-human friendships.

The Nearness Factor

Genuine friendships include a mutual desire for nearness. Following our engagement, my fiancée and I agonized for nearly two years over our frequent separations from each other while we were completing our studies at geographically distant schools.

There is a nearly inconceivable nearness that exists between Christ and his followers. Years ago, I learned a chorus that states this amazing truth: "Near, so very near to God; nearer I could not be. For, in the person of His Son, I am as near as He. Dear, so very dear to God; dearer I could not be. For in the person of His Son, I am as dear as He."[47]

Followers of Jesus are, in a positional sense, as near to God the Father as is Jesus himself! Scripture leaves no room for doubt. They are "seated with him in the heavenly realms,"[48] and Jesus is "at the right hand of the throne of God."[49] That God-human nearness will be more fully realized when we become "away from the body and at home with the Lord"[50]—or when God comes down to make his dwelling among men: "He will live with them ... and God himself will be with them."[51]

God's desire for nearness to his human creation is one

of the most amazing and important truths we can know about him. Jesus died to remove the distance between an infinitely holy God and a sinful human race.

The Bible is a progressive revelation of God's desire for human companions. It is an amazing story. It began in the Garden of Eden and will conclude with a triumphant wedding celebration.

Throughout history, the God who walked with Adam and Eve in Eden has continued seeking people with whom he can have companionship. Early in scripture, we are introduced to two companions of God. The first was Enoch: "Enoch was taken from this life, so that he did not experience death; he could not be found, because God had taken him away. For before he was taken, he was commended as one who pleased God."[52]

How did Enoch please God? The Bible gives only one explanation: "Enoch walked with God."[53]

Later, when God's judgment was about to be rained down on the whole earth, "Noah found favor in the eyes of the Lord."[54] How did Noah find favor with God? The Bible gives only one explanation: "[Noah] walked with God."[55]

When the Lord brought his people out of Egypt, he had in mind more than their deliverance from Egyptian bondage. He was bringing them to himself. He said to Israel, "You yourselves have seen what I did to Egypt, and how I carried you on eagles' wings and brought you to myself .... You will be my treasured possession."[56]

To Joshua, God said, "As I was with Moses, so I will be with you; I will never leave you nor forsake you."[57]

When Solomon dedicated the temple in Jerusalem, he

prayed, "But will God really dwell on earth? The heavens, even the highest heaven, cannot contain you. How much less this temple I have built!"[58]

Solomon's temple was possibly the costliest building ever constructed on earth. "One estimate suggests that the cost of building the temple would be around $3 billion in today's dollars."[59] Nevertheless, Solomon was right when he acknowledged that even such a building was unworthy as a dwelling place of God.

But if Solomon's temple was unworthy of God, how much less worthy was that humble tabernacle in the wilderness—a mere tent covered in animal skins! That tent was called "the Tent of Meeting" because the Lord said, "There I will meet you and speak to you."[60] How incredible! The Living God became a tent dweller for the sake of being among his people!

Solomon's temple and that tent in the wilderness were permeated with the presence of God. The Bible says the glory of the Lord filled both of those places.[61] Even the loaves of bread on display in the holy place were called "the bread of the Presence."[62]

The New Testament introduces us to Jesus by telling us his God-given name, "'Immanuel'—which means 'God with us.'"[63] God was now with humankind not only in the "cool of the day," as he was with Adam and Eve. And not only in the tabernacle and temple where a veil stood between himself and humankind. God, in the person of his Son, took a human body and for thirty-three years lived among us in unprecedented closeness.

But it was a closeness rejected by the people among whom he lived. His grief over their rejection is reflected in these words: "O Jerusalem, Jerusalem, you who kill the prophets and stone those sent to you, how often I have longed to gather your children together, as a hen gathers her chicks under her wings, but you were not willing."[64]

It is the same depth of grief we saw in Genesis, chapter 6, where God was heartbroken over his estranged relationship with humankind.

One of the amazing attributes of God is his desire for closeness to his human creation and his grief when such closeness is rejected.

As Christ's earthly years were coming to an end, he comforted his disciples with these words: "In my Father's house are many rooms .... I am going there to prepare a place for you. And if I go and prepare a place for you, I will come back and take you to be with me that you also may be where I am."[65]

The night before his crucifixion, he prayed, "Father, I want those you have given me to be with me where I am."[66]

To a dying thief, he said, "Today you will be with me in paradise."[67]

Scripture assures us that God's promise to ancient Israel is valid for followers of Christ: "I will never leave you nor forsake you."[68]

When Christ told his disciples to go into all the world and make disciples of all the nations, he comforted them with this promise: "I am with you always, to the very end of the age."[69] His global mission would be accomplished by people to whom he could say, "I am with you."

The mission of God involves a two-way companionship.

It is not only God with us. It is us with him. The mission not only satisfies God's desire for human companionships but at the same time satisfies a human desire for nearness to him. To illustrate this human desire for nearness to Christ, let me give you the testimonies of two of Christ's human lovers.

I heard the late Dr. V. Raymond Edman, longtime president of Wheaton College, pray this prayer: "Lord Jesus, make thyself to me, a living, bright reality; more present to faith's vision keen, than any earthly object seen; more dear, more intimately nigh, then e'en the dearest earthly tie."

While in prison for the sake of Christ, Samuel Rutherford prayed this prayer: "O my Lord Jesus Christ, if I could be in heaven without Thee, it would be hell; and if I could be in hell, and have Thee still, it would be heaven to me, for Thou are all the heaven I want."[70]

Jesus and his human lovers. Mutual joy in each other's presence!

The mission of God is prompted in part by his desire for nearness to his human creation. It's a truth of staggering dimension, but even in our limited understanding, we can marvel at it. It's a mission that will be fully accomplished when at last he has brought to himself people from every ethnic nation on earth.

The Fellowship Factor

Genuine friendships also include fellowship. So it is with God-human friendships. "God is faithful, by whom you were called into the fellowship of his Son, Jesus Christ our Lord."[71]

The apostle John wrote of God-human fellowship, "If we walk in the light, as he is in the light, we have fellowship with one another."[72] Some interpret this text to be speaking of fellowship that exists between Christians. But the context more likely indicates fellowship between the one who is light and those who walk in the light.[73]

We grieve the Lord when, like Martha of old, we are so busy serving him that we haven't time for adequate fellowship with him.[74]

Two-way fellowship! God with us, and we with him. Following Christ's ascension into heaven, he continued to invite such fellowship. From heaven, he said, "I stand at the door and knock. If anyone hears my voice and opens the door, I will come in and eat with him, and he with me."[75]

Christ was speaking figuratively of the open-hearted fellowship friends enjoy when they gather around a table for a meal. Someone has said, "You never really get into a person's heart until you get your feet under their table."

History will conclude with a meal hosted by Christ himself. It is called "the wedding supper of the Lamb." It's an invitation-only meal: "Blessed are those who are invited to the wedding supper of the Lamb!"[76] Who are the invitees? The preceding Bible text identifies them as "a great multitude."[77] Scripture elsewhere describes that great multitude as people from every ethnic nation on earth.[78]

Never was fellowship so sweet as that which will

occur at that wedding feast. Fellowship between Christ and that multiethnic multitude!

The Family Factor

Can it be true that God seeks a human family? When Christ taught his disciples a model prayer, he told them to begin that prayer with the words "Our Father."[79]

There are two human relationships that are unrivaled in terms of person-to-person intimacy. One is marriage. The other is family. God uses both of them to speak of the intimate relationship he desires with humankind.

Christ's suffering was for the purpose of "bringing many sons to glory."[80] Christ spoke of his followers as "my brother and sister and mother,"[81] and scripture repeatedly refers to Christ's followers as "sons [children] of God."[82] Followers of Jesus are called "heirs of God and co-heirs with Christ."[83]

For non-Christians, it can be uncomfortable and unnatural to speak to God in what may seem to them an overfamiliar way. But people who have been born into the family of God[84] take great delight in their father-child relationship to him. The Holy Spirit creates in them a completely natural inclination to call him "Abba, father."[85]

That word *abba* was an Aramaic term phonetically easy for small children to pronounce, similar to the English words *daddy* or *papa*. How remarkable it is that God's sons and daughters can comfortably and naturally address him with that tender word!

I heard the testimony of a man who grew up in a non-Christian religious environment, a religion in which no one ever addressed God as their father. But following his birth into the family of God, this man was surprised at how natural it was to speak to God, calling him "Father."

Christ will have a human bride, and God will have a human family. The bride of Christ will be global—the one for whom Jesus paid a global bride price.[86] And the family of God will be global—the one about which he said to Abraham, "All peoples on earth will be blessed through you."[87]

The Indwelling Factor

We now come to the pinnacle of biblical truth relating to the God–human relationship. Scripture calls it a "profound mystery."[88] There is, in fact, no human person–to–person relationship comparable to that which exists between God and his human lovers.

God is not content with mere human friendships, or human sons and daughters, or face-to-face nearness to humankind. He desires a relationship even more wonderful than that which is pictured by marriage. How so? Marriage speaks of a loving companionship in which two people become intimately bonded to each other. But Christ spoke of a relationship in which he and his human lovers take up residence *within each other.*

Something truly momentous happened following Christ's return to heaven. Upon his arrival in heaven, he asked his Father for the single most transformative thing that can ever happen to a human being. He asked his Father to send the Holy Spirit to indwell the lives of his followers—a relationship in which God in the person of the Holy Spirit would dwell not only *with* people but *in* them. Christ foretold it when he said to his followers, "He [the Holy Spirit] lives with you and will be in you."[89]

Christ asked for a God-human relationship unforeseen and unimagined by any of the Old Testament prophets—a union that did not and could not exist under the Old Testament covenant. That covenant was made in the blood of animals. But the impossible became possible by the shedding of Christ's blood. Only then could there be a complete union of deity and humanity, with each indwelling the other.

Scripture abounds in affirmation of this stunning and unprecedented God-human relationship. Christ said to his disciples, "Remain in me, and I will remain in you."[90] He prayed for his disciples with these words: "Just as you [Father] are in me and I am in you. May they also be in us."[91]

The apostle Paul wrote to Christians at Corinth, "Don't you know that you yourselves are God's temple and that God's Spirit lives in you?"[92] "If anyone is in Christ, he is a new creation."[93]

To Christians at Colossae, Paul wrote, "Christ in you, the hope of glory."[94]

The best protection a follower of Christ has against Satanic power is this: "the one who is in you is greater than the one who is in the world."[95]

Astoundingly, *God yearns to relate to us so intimately that he dwells within us.* But in order for us to relate to him at that level, we must reside in Christ.

What a profound level of God-human intimacy! But

someone may be thinking, *Why am I not experiencing such intimacy in my relationship to God?*

It is important for followers of Jesus to be aware that there can be a difference between their positional relationship to Christ and their experiential relationship to him. Their positional relationship is perfect. Christ is in them, and they are in Christ. They are inseparably bonded to each other. But their experiential relationship to Christ can, at any given time, be less than perfect.

So how can a person have a relationship to Christ that is perfect experientially as well as positionally? Let me share with you how, on one occasion, the Lord made me aware that my experiential relationship to him was not what it needed to be.

One morning years ago, I was pondering these words of Christ: "Whoever believes in me, as the Scripture has said, streams of living water will flow from within him. By this he meant the Spirit, whom those who believed in him were later to receive."[96]

I grieved as I considered that text because I sensed that there were no streams of living water flowing out of me. Trickles, maybe, but not streams. I began praying that the Lord would do anything in me or to me that would enable streams to flow. That has become a lifetime prayer of mine.

It is reassuring to know that it is Christ himself who will complete the mission of God. He declared, "I will build my church, and the gates of Hades will not overcome it."[97]

But the psalmist spoke of the necessary means by which that mission of God will be accomplished: "May

God be gracious to us and bless us and make his face shine upon us, that your ways may be known on earth, your salvation among all nations."[98] Notice the importance of the word *that*. It shows a cause-result relationship between part A and part B of that text. It says salvation will reach all nations by people upon whom the face of God shines. At this hour in history, those are people in whom the Holy Spirit can dwell unstifled and ungrieved.

May we have a vital part in bringing the mission of God to completion by living lives that are an unstifled dwelling place for God the Holy Spirit!

In Summary

Christ has called his followers first and foremost not to a mission but to himself. It is fitting, therefore, that priority be given to the all-important relationship between himself and his human lovers. He has commissioned them with a global mission, but the single most important prerequisite for their involvement in that mission is their maintenance of a vital, personal relationship with the commissioner himself. It is only by means of that relationship that they will be genuinely fruitful in their involvement in that mission. Christ stated it unequivocally: "I am the vine; you are the branches. Whoever abides in me and I in him, he it is that bears much fruit, for apart from me you can do nothing."[99] May the Lord save us from busily producing nothing—toward the advancement of his global mission.

CHAPTER 2

UNIVERSAL WORSHIP

The mission of God includes his pursuit of global worship. It is a mission that will be completed only when heaven will at last resound with a new worship song: "You are worthy ... because you were slain, and with your blood you purchased men for God from every tribe and language and people and nation."[1]

No wonder Christ was furious when he saw what was happening at the temple in Jerusalem. In his fury, he whipped merchants out of the temple and overthrew the tables where they conducted their business. He then explained his anger, saying, "Is it not written: 'my house will be called a house of prayer for all nations'? But you have made it 'a den of robbers.'"[2]

The temple in Jerusalem was a place of worship.[3] It contained a court of the Gentiles, a place specifically reserved for Gentile worshipers. It was that area of the temple that was being defiled by those merchants who cared not at all about God worshipers among Gentile nations. Christ's anger revealed a matter of great importance to him: he wanted worshipers for God not from Israel only but from all nations.

Christ spoke of the day when that temple in Jerusalem would be destroyed, and worship would then emanate not from that physical building but from people's hearts: "True worshipers will worship the Father in spirit and truth, for they are the kind of worshipers the Father seeks."[4]

Have you ever wondered why the mission of God will be accomplished only when there are worshipers for his Son in every language? Why are languages so important to him?

I am familiar with a number of languages and have noticed that each of them has unique features. Some languages, for example, have no abstract nouns, such as the word *faith*. In those languages, abstract concepts are expressed as an action of some kind, languages in which "actions speak louder than words." Or there may be precision in a particular feature of one language that doesn't exist in another language. In English, for example, reference pronouns can sometimes be ambiguous in terms of who or what is being referenced. But in the Duna language of Papua New Guinea, such ambiguity doesn't exist. It is likely that every language has unique strengths and unique weaknesses.

May I dare to say that English is not a totally adequate language in which to worship the Lord? Nor is any other language. God wants his Son to be worshiped by the combined strengths of all the world's languages—a global chorus containing thousands of unique hallelujahs!

It has been instructive to me to gain a biblical

definition of worship. In Old Testament Hebrew, the term *shachah* means to "bow down, prostrate oneself before a monarch or superior [such as] ... before God."[5]

The psalmist wrote, "Come, let us bow down in worship, let us kneel before the Lord our Maker."[6]

King Nebuchadnezzar "bowed to the ground before Daniel and worshiped him."[7] Later, that king issued a proclamation: "This is what you are commanded to do, O peoples, nations and men of every language: You must fall down and worship the image of gold that King Nebuchadnezzar has set up."[8]

When Satan was seeking worship that belonged exclusively to God, he showed Christ "all the kingdoms of the world and their splendor. 'All this I will give you,' he said, 'if you will bow down and worship me.'"[9]

When Job had suffered the loss of virtually everything, "he fell to the ground in worship."[10] Can it be true that the sweetest worship of all is that which is offered to God in the face of crushing circumstances such as Job experienced?

In my college years, I had an occasion to offer the Lord that kind of worship. I was geographically separated from the young lady I loved dearly and hoped one day to marry. But we weren't yet engaged. One day, I received a letter from her, which I wrongly interpreted as a "Dear John" letter. I sensed that she was gently letting me know that there was no future for our romantic relationship.

Fortunately, there was no one nearby when I read that letter, because I wept hard—like I had never wept in my life. Yet, with tears streaming down my cheeks, I lifted my face to heaven and prayed, "Nevertheless, Lord,

I know your will for me is good and perfect, even if it means the ending of this cherished relationship." I even smiled through my tears as I prayed that prayer of simple faith.

My interpretation of that letter was mistaken, and she became my wife—one of the best joys of my life. But I think it was good for the Lord to allow that test in my life, to see if I could trust him enough to worship him in the face of heartbreak. I think that kind of worship is especially precious to the Lord.

Worship is always an act directed to or toward some person or object. It is said that a little girl, when asked, "What is worship?" replied, "It's telling Jesus what we like about him."

It is entirely appropriate for Christians to testify to each other, in word or song, about the worship worthiness of God. The apostle Paul encouraged Christians at Ephesus to "speak to one another with psalms, hymns, and spiritual songs."[11] But he added these words: "Sing and make music in your heart to the Lord."[12] God is honored by what his lovers say *about* him, but he is worshiped by what they say *to* him.

God's pursuit of global worship underlies the mission to which he is committed. God has gone to extravagant lengths to display his glory. Why? Because his glory reveals his worship worthiness.

The Glory of God in the Universe

God created the universe as a stunning display of his glory. "The heavens declare the glory of God; the skies proclaim the work of his hands."[13] "Holy, holy, holy is the Lord Almighty; the whole earth is full of his glory."[14]

Whether viewed through the most powerful telescopes or the most powerful microscopes, or even with the naked eye, all of creation shouts the glory and worship worthiness of its Creator. God intended it to do just that.

Years ago, my wife and I viewed in three dimensions the spectacular film *Hubble*. As we sat in the theater, we were zoomed visually deep into outer space. Stars and planets flew past us at warp speed. I recall seeing in the distance what appeared to be a star. But as we came closer, we found it to be an entire galaxy filled with billions of stars.

No one claims to know the number of stars in the universe. One website (scienceline.org) estimates the existence of "one trillion stars in the observable universe." Another website (space.com) estimates "about two trillion galaxies in the observable universe" and "about 100 million stars in the average galaxy." Another website (skyandtelescope.org) says our own Milky Way galaxy "is home to around 300 billion stars."

As I walked out of the theater that day, I said to my wife, "That was a worship experience!" Indeed, it was! And that is exactly what God intended it to be.

The Glory of God in the Human Body

If we are dazzled by the glory of God displayed in the universe, we should be no less amazed by his glory displayed in a single human body. The facts are utterly mind-boggling. "The human body's cell count is not exactly known. ... According to a recent estimate published in 2013 in 'Annals of Human Biology' by an international team of researchers, the human body consists of some 37.2 trillion cells."[15] Each cell is made up of atoms. How many atoms? "Scientists estimate the average cell [in the human body] contains 100 trillion atoms."[16] In a typical human body, there are seven billion billion billion atoms. That is a seven followed by twenty-seven zeros.[17]

But the display of God's glory in creation is imperfect because all creation has suffered the consequences of humankind's rebellion against God. Creation groans, therefore, for the day when it "will be liberated from its bondage to decay."[18]

Nevertheless, even in its state of decay, creation is a stunning display of the glory of its Creator.

But the glory of God in creation is small by comparison to his glory in redemption.

The Glory of God in Redemption

Not even the worship of angels can match the passionate worship of redeemed sinners. Years ago, I learned the words of a song that speaks of this truth:

> There is singing up in heaven such as we
> have never known,
> Where the angels sing the praises of the
> Lamb upon the throne.

Their sweet harps are ever tuneful and
their voices always clear,
O that we might be more like them while
we serve the Master here!
Holy, holy, is what the angels sing,
And I expect to help them make the
courts of heaven ring;
But when I sing redemption's story, they
will fold their wings.
For angels never felt the joys that our
salvation brings.[19]

Redeemed sinners bring glory to God not only by
their verbal worship but also by their transformed lives. In
some amazing degree, they are remade into the likeness
of God. Scripture describes that transformation process:
"And we, who with unveiled faces all reflect the Lord's
glory, are being transformed into his likeness with ever-
increasing glory."[20] "In all things God works for the good
of those who love him, who have been called ... to be
conformed to the likeness of his Son."[21]

That radical transformation has been beautifully
expressed in the words of this song:

In the image of God we
were made long ago,
with the purpose divine,
here His glory to show.
But we failed Him one day,
and like sheep went astray,

> thinking not of the cost; we
> His likeness had lost.
> But from eternity, God had in mind,
> the work of Calvary, the lost to find.
> From His heaven so broad Christ
> came down, earth to trod,
> so that men might live again in the
> image of God.[22]

When God, in the person of the Holy Spirit, takes up residence in people, a radical character transformation commences. They begin to exhibit Christlike character qualities described as "the fruit of the Spirit." "The fruit of the Spirit is love, joy, peace, patience, kindness, goodness, faithfulness, gentleness and self-control."[23]

Love—where natural love wouldn't exist. Joy—where natural joy would be impossible. Peace—even in the midst of pain. Every one of these Holy Spirit–given character qualities reflects the glory of Christ's own character.

But there is a problem. No follower of Christ can truthfully claim to be perfectly Christlike. Thankfully, that is not the end of the story. Scripture declares that every lover of Christ will one day be transformed fully and perfectly into his image. "Now we are children of God, and what we will be has not yet been made known. But we know that when he [Christ] appears, we shall be like him, for we shall see him as he is."[24]

No miracle of God could be greater than the transformation of sinners into Christlikeness! It is a miracle now in progress in the lives of Christ's human lovers. It is a transformation with a purpose. That purpose was stated by Christ: "Let your light shine before men, that they may see your good deeds and praise your Father in heaven."[25]

Sinners transformed—for the sake of God's glory!

The Glory of God in the Person of Jesus

Because of sin's devastating consequences, the glory of God is currently revealed imperfectly on earth. But there was a short time in human history when God's glory was revealed fully and perfectly on this planet. It was revealed in the person of his Son. Scripture speaks of that glory: "The glory of God in the face of Jesus Christ."[26] "In Christ all the fullness of the Deity lives in bodily form."[27] "[Jesus] is the radiance of God's glory and the exact representation of his being."[28] "Anyone who has seen me has seen the Father,"[29] said Christ.

My parents were pioneer missionaries in northern Ghana. My father shared the Gospel of Christ in numerous villages where no one had ever heard of Jesus. Upon arrival in a village, he would set up a little pump organ in some central location. Then, as my mother began playing that organ, a crowd would gather, and my father would begin telling people about Christ.

My father told of one occasion when, as he was telling people about Christ, he noticed a very old man at the back of the crowd who was listening intently to every word my father said. As usual, at the end of his message, my father invited anyone who wanted to trust in Jesus and become his follower to come and stand with him. Immediately, that old man pushed his way through the crowd and stood next to my father, indicating his desire to become a follower of Jesus.

The old man died not long after that, but before he died, he told everyone in the village of how, for many years, he had been praying to the Great One who had created all things, asking how he could be pleasing to that Creator. As he listened to my father telling about Christ, the Creator-Redeemer, he knew his prayers were answered.

After marveling for years at the glory of the Great One who created all things, he hungered to have a right relationship to the Creator himself. And that day, he became a worshiper of Jesus, the Great One by whom creation came into existence.

The mission of God is about bringing people into a worship relationship to him—by introducing them to Jesus.

Surprises

God sometimes does surprising things for the sake of his glory. Consider the death of Lazarus. Scripture states, "Jesus loved Martha and her sister and Lazarus."[30] Therefore, when Lazarus became sick, Mary and Martha sent word to Christ, confident that Jesus would come quickly and heal their brother. But that didn't happen. Christ intentionally stayed where he was another two days until he knew Lazarus had died. Only then did he come. And it was too late. By that time, Lazarus had been dead four days, and Jesus found everyone in tears. Even Mary and Martha were sure that Jesus had come too late. He could do nothing now except join them in their sorrow.

Here is what strikes me about this account: Jesus intentionally allowed heartbreak in the lives of these whom he loved. He did so for only one reason: the glory of God. While awaiting Lazarus's death, he had explained to his disciples that Lazarus's illness and death were "for God's glory."[31] Later, upon arrival at Lazarus's tomb, Jesus said to Martha, "Did I not tell you that if you believed, you would see the glory of God?"[32]

It was out of Mary and Martha's heartbreak that they and many others saw the glory of God like never before. And many, for the first time, became worshipers of God and his Son.

We shouldn't be surprised or offended if, for the sake of his glory, God allows heartbreak in the lives of those he loves dearly. He does so only because joy ultimately awaits them when they see—whether in time or eternity—how the Lord was glorified by their experience.

God's Glory in the Lives of Christ's Followers

It is widely believed that the apostle Peter died by crucifixion. That seems the best explanation for what the apostle John later wrote concerning Peter's death. John quoted what Christ had said to Peter: "When you were younger you dressed yourself and went where you wanted; but when you are old you will stretch out your hands, and someone else will dress you and lead you where you do not want to go."[33] John then added, "Jesus said this to indicate the kind of death by which Peter would glorify God."[34]

The crucifixion of Peter—for the sake of God's glory!

Christ encountered a beggar who had been blind from birth. Christ's disciples asked him, "Rabbi, who sinned, this man or his parents, that he was born blind?"[35] Jesus replied, "Neither this man nor his parents sinned … but this happened so that the work of God might be displayed in his life."[36] It was that work of God that turned this man into a worshiper of the Lord.[37]

That man's blindness—for the sake of his becoming a worshiper of Jesus.

The glory of God was costly for Philippian Christians who suffered greatly because of their allegiance to Christ. But to them, the apostle Paul wrote, "It has been granted to you that for the sake of Christ you should not only believe in him but also suffer for his sake."[38]

Christians allowed to suffer for the sake of Christ's glory.

The apostle Paul experienced enormous suffering for the sake of Christ, but he summed up his all-consuming passion with these words: "That now as always Christ will be exalted in my body, whether by life or by death."[39] Whether he lived or died was not a primary concern to Paul. The one thing that mattered most to him was the exaltation of Christ.

But that passion was not unique to Paul. Throughout history, there have been millions who, like most of the apostles, willingly forfeited their lives for the sake of Christ's glory. Others have spent their entire lives serving Christ, sometimes in very costly ways. That was true of David Livingstone. As a pioneer missionary to Africa, Livingstone spent his whole adult life often in primitive environments, for the sake of God's glory. These are his words: "I will place no value on anything I have or may possess except in relation to the kingdom of Christ. If anything will advance the interests of His kingdom, it shall be given away or kept, only as by given or kept it will most promote the glory of Him to whom I owe all my hopes in time and eternity."[40]

Like David Livingston, many others have lived their entire lives to promote the glory and worship worthiness of Christ—often in places where no such worship had ever existed.

The glory of God should be the central passion of all followers of Christ. The apostle Paul wrote, "Whether you eat or drink or whatever you do, do it all for the glory of God."[41] Whatever you do! What a mandate! What a reflection of Christ's own life!

Jesus urged his disciples to stay intimately connected to him, saying, "If a man remains in me and I in him, he will bear much fruit ... This is to my Father's glory, that you bear much fruit."[42] An intimate relationship to Jesus—the only means by which a Christian can bear fruit and, in so doing, glorify God.

We might well ask ourselves how important God's glory is to us. Is there any price too high for us to pay for the sake of his glory? For me, it has been important to pray, "Lord, honor yourself in my life by any means you choose." That's a risky prayer. It requires me to hold with an open hand every precious thing and person in my life, offering them unreservedly to the Lord—so that whether I keep them or lose them, he will be most glorified.

If we are to bring our lives into harmony with the

mission of God, his global glory and worship must be a core purpose for our existence. Only as we embrace that passion will we go wherever we need to go and do whatever we need to do to make disciples—worshipers for God—in every ethnic nation on earth.

What Matters Most to Jesus

No one ever cared so much about the glory of God as did Jesus. Here are his words as he neared the time of his crucifixion: "Now my heart is troubled, and what shall I say? 'Father, save me from this hour'? No, it is for this very reason I came to this hour. Father, glorify your name!"[43]

Christ's crucifixion was the staggering price he willingly paid—for the sake of God's glory.

When I became engaged to the young lady I would one day marry, I was a student at Wheaton College in Wheaton, Illinois. I was financially unable at that time to give her a diamond engagement ring, but together we inspected rings at a local jeweler. That is how I knew the style of ring she wanted.

The following summer, I worked exceptionally long hours at a local store and was finally able to purchase a diamond engagement ring. I later mentioned to a friend that I had bought the ring from a local jeweler. He told me, "You could have purchased a diamond ring much cheaper in downtown Chicago."

But I was leery about jewelers in downtown Chicago. Too many had a bad reputation. Therefore, I knowingly paid a higher price, buying a ring from a local jeweler. I knew he would not risk his reputation by selling a diamond of poor quality. It was from that experience that my life's motto became "No cheap diamonds for Jesus!"

There was nothing cheap about the price Jesus paid to purchase worshipers for God. He purchased them by taking their sins on himself and experiencing the anguish of separation from his Father. Who can comprehend the trauma of that Father–Son separation? It was a soul-wrenching experience, causing Jesus to cry out, "My God, my God, why have you forsaken me?"[44]

Christ's trauma was especially excruciating in view of their Father–Son relationship that existed from eternity past, a relationship in which Jesus had lived "in the bosom of the Father."[45]

In our day, we don't speak of bosoms in the same way scripture uses that term. Most modern translations, therefore, provide an interpretation of that term rather than a literal translation. For that reason, I have quoted the literal rendering as it appears in the New American Standard Bible.

What did it mean for Jesus to exist "in the bosom of the Father"? In Bible times, a shepherd with an exceptionally tender relationship to a particular lamb might carry that lamb in his arms.[46]

Commentaries agree that this bosom relationship between the Father and his Son speaks of the Father's tender love for his Son. Imagine, therefore, the profound heartbreak Christ experienced when "the Lord laid on him [Jesus] the iniquity of us all"[47] and "Christ redeemed us from the curse of the law by becoming a curse for us."[48]

Having always lived in the most intimate relationship to his Father, it was the Father's curse that crushed him.

The complete achievement of God's glory required the blood sacrifice of his Son. To Jesus, the glory of his Father was worth that enormous price.

Besides Jesus's determined commitment to the Father's glory, he was also jealous for the honor and glory that belongs to the third member of the Godhead: "Every sin and blasphemy will be forgiven men, but the blasphemy against the Spirit will not be forgiven. Anyone who speaks a word against the Son of Man will be forgiven, but anyone who speaks against the Holy Spirit will not be forgiven, either in this age or in the age to come."[49]

What Matters Most to God the Father

Ultimate glory for God the Father awaits the universal exaltation of his Son. Notice how Christ's exaltation brings glory to his Father: "God exalted him [Jesus] to the highest place and gave him the name that is above every name, that at the name of Jesus every knee should bow, in heaven and on earth and under the earth, and every tongue confess that Jesus Christ is Lord, to the glory of God the Father."[50]

A question arises from the above text: when every knee bows to Jesus, is that an act of voluntary worship or only mandatory submission? That question can be debated. But whatever it signifies, it is an act that exalts Christ. And when that happens, God the Father will receive glory. How so? Because despite fierce Satanic and demonic opposition, God will at last successfully accomplish the universal exaltation of his Son. All-inclusive is the phrase "in heaven and on earth and under the earth." It includes angels and demons, the living and the dead, the saved and the lost. No one anywhere will be exempt from exalting Jesus, bowing their knees to him.

The honor and glory of Jesus is of utmost importance to his Father. Christ described it this way: "The Father ... has entrusted all judgment to the Son, that all may honor the Son just as they honor the Father."[51]

The honor and glory of Jesus is a gift from the Father to his Son: "Father, I want those you have given me to be with me where I am, and to see my glory, the glory you have given me because you loved me before the creation of the world."[52]

God the Father has commanded angels to worship his Son: "When God brings his firstborn into the world, he says, 'Let all God's angels worship him.'"[53]

Twice during Christ's earthly ministry God audibly honored Jesus by calling him "my Son." The first instance was at Christ's baptism when God proclaimed from heaven, "This is my Son, whom I love; with him I am well pleased."[54] Again, when Christ was transfigured before three of his disciples, the voice of God from the clouds declared, "This is my Son whom I love."[55]

These New Testament texts record what God said *about* Jesus. But the psalmist quoted what God the Father said *to* Jesus, declaring, "You are my Son."[56]

What did it mean to Jesus for his Father to publicly honor him by calling him "my Son"?

I am reminded of my own relationship to my son. He is one of my best earthly joys. So, in environments where people have known me but not him, it has always been a delight for me to introduce him as "my son." But in environments where people knew him but not me, he has been pleased to introduce me as "my father." That is how it has been with God the Father and his Son. Christ frequently spoke of God as "my Father," and God was pleased to identify Jesus as "my Son."

Why does the honor of Jesus mean so much to his Father? In partial answer to that question, I recall times in my life when I was publicly honored. No one in the audience was more pleased than my wife. She loved me and loved seeing me honored. Such will be the case when at last God the Father sees his dearly loved Son receive universal honor. Imagine the Father's joy when he sees that happen!

The honor of Jesus is of paramount importance to his Father. The global mission of God is driven in part by the Father's desire for the whole world to know that Jesus is his Son—and in that knowledge, for people of every ethnic nation to become worshipers of his Son.

What Matters Most to the Holy Spirit

There is a beautiful relationship between the three members of the deity—Father, Son, and Holy Spirit. As noted earlier, Jesus is committed to the honor and glory of his Father, and God the Father is committed to the honor and glory of Jesus. Likewise, the Holy Spirit is committed to the honor and glory of Jesus. Christ testified of that truth when speaking to his disciples about the ministry of the Holy Spirit: "When he, the Spirit of truth, comes ... He will bring glory to me by taking from what is mine and making it known to you."[57]

One means by which the Holy Spirit glorifies Jesus is by creating Christlikeness in Jesus's followers. As noted earlier, that Christlikeness is called "the fruit of the Spirit."

I heard the story of a godly man who was dining with friends at a restaurant. It was a formal event, with everyone dressed for the occasion. A waitress accidentally spilled coffee down the front of this man's suit and necktie. She was mortified. But he immediately exclaimed, "I am so sorry this has happened to you!" That waitress was aware that people at that table were followers of Christ. And that man, by his kindness, gentleness, and self-control, glorified Jesus in the eyes of that waitress. That is what the Holy Spirit does in the lives of Christ's followers.

In addition to creating Christlikeness in the lives of Jesus followers, the Holy Spirit also prompts people to verbally glorify Jesus. That happened as Stephen was being stoned to death: "But Stephen, full of the Holy Spirit, looked up to heaven and saw the glory of God, and Jesus standing at the right hand of God. 'Look,' he said, 'I see heaven open and the Son of Man standing at the right hand of God.'"[58]

The apostle Peter exalted Christ when he was brought before a hostile gathering of Jewish leaders. When those leaders demanded to know by what power or by what name Peter had healed a man who had been lame from birth, Peter's reply was prompted by the Holy Spirit: "Peter, filled with the Holy Spirit, said … 'Rulers and elders of the people! … Know this: … It is by the name of Jesus Christ of Nazareth whom you crucified but whom God raised from the dead, that this man stands before you healed.'"[59]

"James McConkey said at one time that he believed that a few men had a monopoly on the Holy Spirit. 'But now,' he said, 'I know that the Holy Spirit has a monopoly on a few men.'"[60]

One primary characteristic of people on whom the Holy Spirit has a monopoly is their consuming desire to see Jesus glorified.

What Mattered Most to the Psalm Writers

God's glory is a central theme of the book of Psalms. Here are some of the psalmists' statements:

"Lord, our Lord, how majestic is your name in all the earth! You have set your glory above the heavens."[61]

"The heavens declare the glory of God; the skies proclaim the work of his hands."[62]

"Lift up your heads, O you gates; lift them up, you ancient doors, that the King of glory may come in. Who is he, this King of glory? The Lord Almighty – he is the King of glory."[63]

"Ascribe to the Lord, O mighty ones, ascribe to the Lord glory and strength. Ascribe to the Lord the glory due his name."[64]

"Be exalted, O God, above the heavens; let your glory be over all the earth."[65]

"O, God, you are my God ... Because your love is better than life, my lips will glorify you."[66]

"Praise be to the Lord God, the God of Israel .... Praise be to his glorious name forever; may the whole earth be filled with his glory."[67]

"Help us, O God our Savior, for the glory of your name."[68]

"O Lord ... let our children see your glory at work."[69]

"Sing to the Lord, all the earth .... Declare his glory among the nations, his marvelous deeds among all peoples."[70]

"Ascribe to the Lord, O families of nations, ascribe to the Lord glory and strength. Ascribe to the Lord the glory due his name."[71]

"The nations will fear the name of the Lord, all the kings of the earth will revere your glory."[72]

"May the glory of the Lord endure forever."[73]

"Be exalted, O God, above the heavens, and let your glory be over all the earth."[74]

"The Lord is exalted over all the nations, his glory above the heavens."[75]

"Not to us, O Lord, not to us but to your name be the glory."[76]

"May all the kings of the earth praise you, O Lord .... May they sing of the ways of the Lord, for the glory of the Lord is great."[77]

Notice the frequent occurrence of these phrases throughout the above texts: "all the earth"; "the whole earth"; "the nations"; "all people"; "families of nations"; "all the kings of the earth"; "all the nations."

The psalmists wanted the glory and worship worthiness of God to be made known throughout the whole earth and among all ethnic peoples. It was the psalmists' passion, and it needs to be ours as well.

Warfare of the Ages

A monumental war is raging on planet Earth. In the words of the late Saddam Hussein, it might be called "the mother of all wars." The war is about worship and who receives it: God or his archenemy, Satan.

Satan knows what is in the Bible and was able to quote scripture when he was tempting Christ in the wilderness. It is because of Satan's Bible knowledge that he is aware of the fate that ultimately awaits him. Not only does he know his fate, but he knows what must happen before he meets his fate: "This gospel of the kingdom will be preached in the whole world as a testimony to all nations, and then the end will come."[78] A parallel text in the Gospel of Mark says, "The gospel must first be preached to all nations."[79]

Global proclamation of the Gospel is an important signal that will tell Satan when time is running out for him. And he knows from scripture the horror that awaits him. No wonder scripture informs us that when he sees his time is growing short, he will be filled with great wrath: "But woe to the earth and the sea, because the devil has gone down to you! He is filled with fury, because he knows that his time is short."[80]

The global mission of God will be accomplished in the face of intense Satanic opposition. His opposition stems from his desire to rob God of worship and gain that worship for himself. Never was that more evident than when he was tempting Christ in the wilderness. Here is the record of that temptation: "The devil led him [Jesus] up to a high place and showed him in an instant all the kingdoms of the world. And he said to him [Jesus], 'I will give you all their authority and splendor, for it has been given to me, and I can give it to anyone I want to. So if you worship me, it will all be yours.'"[81]

Notice the intensity of Satan's desire for worship. He marshalled every resource at his disposal to tempt Jesus. Why? Because if he could gain the worship of the Son of God, it would be the ultimate coup d'état!

As the end of the age approaches, this Satanic passion will be revealed in the person of Satan's chief emissary, the antichrist: "He will oppose and will exalt himself over everything that is called God or is worshiped, so that he sets himself up in God's temple, proclaiming himself to be God."[82]

In eternity past, God in his foreknowledge knew what would happen if he created humankind. He knew humankind would rebel against him and that reconciliation between himself and sinners would require the sacrificial death of his Son. This raises a question: why did God create humankind, knowing what that God-human reconciliation would cost him? The answer to that question has everything to do with God's pursuit of worship: there is no worship so passionate as the worship of redeemed sinners. God already has universal worship in heaven, but he seeks the uniquely passionate worship of sinners who have been purchased for God at the cost of Christ's blood.

Some might ask if it is appropriate for God to seek honor and glory for himself—because, in fact, we tend to shun people who seek glory for themselves. How, then, can it be legitimate for God to seek glory for himself? The answer is unmistakable. When we seek glory for ourselves, we seek what doesn't belong to us. Our sin makes us worthy of condemnation, not glory. But when God seeks glory for himself, he does so in perfect righteousness, seeking only what rightly and exclusively belongs to him.

But God's pursuit of worship sets the stage for this epic war between the kingdom of God and the kingdom of Satan. That war has been in progress throughout history. It is a war in which Satan is passionately devoted to robbing God of worship.

It is comforting for followers of Jesus to know how this war ends. I heard the testimony of a man who grew up in Atlanta and never heard the Gospel until he was forty years of age. But the first time he heard the Gospel, he put his trust in Christ. He had no one to disciple him but somehow knew he should be reading the Bible. So he bought a Bible. He didn't know where to begin reading, so he began with the book of Revelation. He said, "I have never regretted reading the book of Revelation first, because I found out how things are going to turn out in the end. And I've been an optimist ever since!"

We have every reason to be optimistic because we know from scripture how this war will end. Satan, archenemy of God, will be defeated and consigned to an eternal lake of fire. And there will at last be passionate worshipers for the Lord from every ethnic nation on earth.

Meanwhile, the war remains furiously in progress. It began in the Garden of Eden, where Satan successfully lured Adam and Eve into rebellion against God. The war continued in Satan's attempts to destroy Israel, the nation of whom God said, "[Israel] whom I created for my glory."[83]

Israel was—and will once again become—the epicenter of global worship for God. It is not surprising, therefore, that the very survival of the world's Jews has been threatened repeatedly throughout history. No example is more spectacular than that which occurred in the days of Queen Esther, when the annihilation of the Jews was imminent. Only by a series of amazing divine interventions were the Jews of the vast Persian Empire saved from perishing.

Only by angelic intervention was Christ (the ultimate Seed of Abraham) saved from murder at the hands of wicked King Herod.

As Christ's earthly ministry was nearing an end, it was Satan himself who put it in the heart of Judas Iscariot to betray Christ with a kiss.[84]

Satan despises Israel primarily because he despises Israel's preeminent Son, Jesus, who will one day be given the glory and worship so earnestly coveted by Satan.

Satan remains on the warpath to this day and continues doing everything in his power to rob God of worship. And he has a multitude of successes. Speaking of humankind in general, the apostle Paul wrote, "Although they knew God, they neither glorified him as God nor gave thanks to him ... They exchanged the truth of God for a lie, and worshiped and served created things rather than the Creator."[85]

Satan's fury will reach maximum intensity as this age nears an end. Followers of Christ will face unprecedented fury from this chief enemy of God because he hates both the worship and the worshipers of God. That may not be a comforting truth, but we do well to be aware of it.

But Satanic opposition, fierce though it may be, is not the end of the story. The mission of God will at last be completed, resulting in eternal worship for him. John Piper has stated this truth succinctly: "Missions is not the ultimate goal of the Church. Worship is. Missions exists where worship doesn't .... When this age is over ... missions will be no more. It is a temporary necessity. But worship abides forever."[86]

I have often sung the words of this chorus: "Father, we love you; we worship and adore you. Glorify your name in all the earth!"[87] But there came into my life an event that nearly crushed me, and I found it hard to sing that chorus. I was forced to question whether God's glory was so important to me that it was worth whatever it might cost me. But at last I was able to pray, "Lord, glorify yourself in my life by absolutely any means you choose." I am trusting the Lord to enable me to continue with that commitment regardless of whatever circumstances I may face in the future.

Concerning this raging war that affects the lives of followers of Christ, it may appear from time to time that Satan has created truly impenetrable strongholds. But we need not lose heart because we know from scripture that Christ will one day be known and worshiped in every ethnic nation on earth. Importantly, he has given us a mandate to join him in making that happen.

In Summary

Our culture is full of expressions like "self-fulfillment," "self-esteem," "self-awareness"—reflecting our tendency to be self-centered. But if we are to bring our lives into harmony with the mission of God, his global glory and worship must be a core purpose for our existence.

CHAPTER 3

A SOLEMN OATH

God swears—not profanely but in affirmation of certain promises he has made. Why, then, did Christ say to his disciples, "Don't swear!"? It is because only God is able, without any possibility of failure, to accomplish what he has promised by oath.

The promises of God contained in scripture can be divided into three major categories: usual promises, covenant promises, and oath promises. All of God's promises are reliable, because as scripture says, "It is impossible for God to lie."[1] But the unique solemnity of God's *oath promises* can be fully appreciated only when viewed within the context of God's other promises. For that reason, we will first consider God's other promises.

Usual Promises of God

The Bible abounds with promises of God. How many? Dr. Everek R. Storms of Ontario, Canada, spent a vast amount of time studying the promises of scripture. Writing in

Contact magazine, he said, "The Holy Scriptures contain a grand total of 8,810 promises. How do I know? I counted them." He went on to say, "There are 7,487 promises from God to man."[2]

I heard the late Vance Havner say, "Stop sitting on the premises and start standing on the promises!" Happy are those who learn to do just that!

The apostle Peter described God's promises as "very great and precious."[3] Here is a sampling of those promises:

"I know the plans I have for you, declares the Lord, plans to prosper you and not to harm you, plans to give you hope and a future."[4]

"Though the mountains be shaken and the hills be removed, yet my unfailing love for you will not be shaken nor my covenant of peace be removed, says the Lord, who has compassion on you."[5]

"Do not fear, for I am with you; do not be dismayed, for I am your God. I will strengthen you and help you; I will uphold you with my righteous right hand."[6]

"My sheep listen to my voice; I know them, and they follow me. I give them eternal life, and they shall never perish; no one can snatch them out of my hand."[7]

"I will instruct you and teach you in the way you should go; I will counsel you with my eye upon you."[8]

The Bible is an overflowing warehouse of such assurances for those who love and follow the Lord.

But not all of God's promises are assurances of his blessing. Sixteen times God's promise is preceded with the words "As surely as I live ..." In every case, they are promises of God's judgment on Israel or on Israel's enemies, or, in one case, a promise that assures universally required subservience to Jesus. None of them are promises of blessing. Here is a sampling of those promises:

"As surely as I live ... not one of the men who saw my glory and the miraculous signs I performed in Egypt ... not one of them will ever see the land I promised on oath to their forefathers."[9]

"'As surely as I live,' declares the Lord, ... 'I will hand you over to those who seek your life, those you fear—to Nebuchadnezzar king of Babylon and to the Babylonians.'"[10]

"'As surely as I live,' declares the King, whose name is the Lord Almighty ... The Daughter of Egypt will be put to shame, handed over to the people of the north.'"[11]

"As surely as I live, declares the Sovereign Lord ... The soul who sins is the one who will die."[12]

"It is written: 'As surely as I live,' says the Lord, 'every knee will bow before me; every tongue will confess to God.'"[13]

Nevertheless, whatever the nature of God's promises, they are assured of fulfillment because God is as good as his word.

Years ago, I heard the late Don Richardson tell of a conversation he had with a Jewish rabbi. Don asked the rabbi, "What is the significance in Hebrew Scriptures when God repeats the same statement three times?" The rabbi replied, "That happens only once in our scriptures. Three times God commands us not to boil a young goat in its mother's milk. We don't understand why that is important to God, but that threefold repetition tells us it must be important to him, so we take that command very seriously."

Don then asked the rabbi, "What is the significance in Hebrew scriptures when God repeats the same statement five times?" The rabbi replied, "That never happens in our scriptures." Don then showed him these five statements in which God promised to bless all ethnic nations through Abraham's offspring:

To Abraham, God said, "I will bless you ... so that you will be a blessing. ... and in you all the families of the earth shall be blessed."[14]

Concerning Abraham, God said, "All nations on earth will be blessed through him."[15]

To Abraham, God repeated, "Through your offspring all nations on earth will be blessed."[16]

To Isaac, Abraham's son, God said, "Through your offspring all nations on earth will be blessed."[17]

To Jacob, Abraham's grandson, God said, "I am the LORD, the God of your father Abraham and the God of Isaac ... All peoples on earth will be blessed through you and your offspring."[18]

The rabbi was surprised and said he had never noticed these repetitions of God's promise of global blessing through Abraham's descendants.

Among other things, the mission of God is about his faithfulness in keeping this repeated promise of global blessing through Abraham's descendants.

Covenant Promises of God

Because God never lies, there is no need for any special assurance that he will fulfill what he has promised. But on occasion, God made his promises doubly sure by means of a formal covenant. Although there is no consensus on the number of covenants in the Bible, five such covenants are of special importance.

The first of those covenants is the one God made with Noah. God said to him, "I establish my covenant with you: Never again will all life be cut off by the waters of a flood; never again will there be a flood to destroy the earth."[19]

The second covenant is the one God made with Abraham. It has been called the most important and determinative revelation of scripture.[20]

The third covenant is the one God made with the nation of Israel. Speaking of that covenant, scripture says, "Moses summoned all the Israelites and said to them ... 'Carefully follow the terms of this covenant, so that you may prosper in everything you do.'"[21]

The fourth covenant of God is the one he made with David. David spoke of that covenant, saying, "Is not my house right with God? Has he not made with me an everlasting covenant?"[22] In further affirmation of that Davidic covenant, God said to Solomon, "As for you, if you walk before me as David your father did ... I will establish your royal throne, as I covenanted with David your father when I said, 'You shall never fail to have a man to rule over Israel.'"[23]

A fifth promise is the one made in Christ's blood. It is called a "new covenant"[24] and a "better covenant"[25]— superior to all previous blood sacrifices that required endless repetitions. Christ's was a once-for-all sacrifice that did what no other blood sacrifice had done. It "put away sin."[26] This is the one and only covenant that assures eternal life for every follower of Christ.

The profound significance of the Abrahamic covenant is revealed progressively in the early chapters of Genesis. In chapter 12, the covenant is simply announced. In chapter 15, it is depicted as an unconditional promise. In chapters 17 and 18, it is mentioned again, and in chapter 22, God repeats it yet again. Here are details relating to each of those progressive revelations:

In chapter 12, God's promise to Abraham includes a fivefold repetition of the phrase "I will," indicating that God is taking completely on himself the responsibility of keeping that covenant.

The fifteenth chapter of Genesis describes the stunning way in which God committed himself unconditionally to fulfilling that covenant. He used a procedure consistent with the cultural norms of that day—a procedure in which animals were cut in half, with the two halves separated from each other and facing each other. Persons who made that covenantal promise would then pass between those separated animal parts. Such a ceremony was called "cutting a covenant." It refers to the butchering of the victims that were slain in the ceremony attendant upon concluding a covenant. The significance of that solemn act may have implied that a fate similar to the fate of those animals would befall anyone who violated that covenant.[27]

Covenants were normally a mutual agreement between two individual parties, both of whom passed between those animal parts. But God's covenant with Abraham was a unilateral and unconditional covenant in which he alone passed between those animal parts, thus assuring Abraham that the fulfillment of that covenant was a one-way commitment on his part, with no obligation whatsoever on Abraham's part.

But a promise is only as reliable as the one who makes it. Notice, therefore, that God passed between the slain animals in the image of "a smoking firepot with a blazing torch."[28] Such an image is not a surprising representation of God. On other occasions, he appeared to Moses in the form of a burning bush,[29] and on Mount Sinai as a smoking fire,[30] and throughout Israel's wilderness wanderings as a "pillar of fire."[31] All of these images were stunning representations of an awesome God. Thus, God's covenant with Abraham was assured of fulfillment because of who made that covenant—the awesome God himself!

Oath Promises of God

Among the thousands of God's promises, there are none so solemn as the ones he made with an oath. The Bible records only seven occasions when God swore with an oath, although some of those are mentioned more than once. Here are those seven oaths:

This was God's oath to Abraham: "By myself I have sworn, declares the Lord, because you have done this and have not withheld your son, your only son, I will surely bless you and in your offspring shall all the nations of the earth be blessed, because you have obeyed my voice."[32]

This was God's oath to David: "I have made a

covenant with my chosen one, I have sworn to David my servant, 'I will establish your line forever.'"[33]

This was God's oath regarding Israelites while they were wandering in the wilderness: "When the Lord heard what you said, he was angry and solemnly swore: 'Not a man of this evil generation shall see the good land I swore to give your forefathers, except Caleb.'"[34]

This was God's oath regarding the northern kingdom of Israel: "The Lord has sworn by the pride of Jacob: 'Surely I will never forget any of their deeds.' Shall not the land tremble on this account, and everyone mourn who dwells in it?"[35]

This was God's oath to the southern kingdom of Judah while exiled in Babylon: "I gave you my solemn oath and entered into a covenant with you, declares the Sovereign Lord, and you became mine ... But you trusted in your beauty and used your fame to become a prostitute .... I will deal with you as you deserve, because you have despised my oath by breaking the covenant."[36]

This was God's oath regarding Judah's future: "The Lord has sworn by his right hand and by his mighty arm: 'Never again will I give your grain as food for your enemies.'"[37]

This was God's oath regarding Christ: "Others became priests without any oath, but he [Christ] became a priest with an oath when God said to him: 'The Lord has sworn and will not change his mind: You are a priest forever.'"[38]

This was God's oath promising universal allegiance to him: "By myself I have sworn, my mouth has uttered in all integrity a word that will not be revoked: Before me every knee will bow."[39]

Of all these oaths of God, two are exceptionally solemn, introduced with this phrase: "By myself I have sworn."

Christ's oath, as recorded by Isaiah, is of enormous significance. It has to do with the inheritance Jesus will ultimately receive, an inheritance in which every knee will bow before him. But that is a topic for another chapter in this book. For the purpose of this chapter, God's oath to Abraham is of special interest because it promises blessing not only for Israel but for all nations on earth. It is an oath mentioned forty times throughout the Bible.

In an American court of law, witnesses may be required to raise their right hand and swear to "tell the truth, the whole truth, and nothing but the truth." But God's oath to Abraham was of greater solemnity than that. This is how scripture describes it: "When God made a promise to Abraham, since he had no one greater by whom to swear, he swore by himself ... an oath is final for confirmation ... it is impossible for God to lie."[40]

Concerning this oath, one highly credible commentator has written, "Jehovah swore by Himself, a thing which never occurs again in His intercourse with the patriarchs."[41]

The Oath's Requirements

The fulfillment of God's oath to Abraham required these achievements:

1. Abraham's descendants must be preserved throughout history as a distinct ethnic people.
2. A Jewish nation must one day come into existence on land that for two thousand years was largely and zealously occupied by non-Jews.
3. Through Abraham's offspring, blessing must reach every ethnic nation on earth.

Consider now the unlikely possibility that these three achievements would ever be accomplished:

1. A preserved ethnic identity

Three times throughout history, the Jews have been forcibly scattered among Gentile nations.

"In 722 BC, the Assyrians conquered Israel .... When they conquered Israel, they forced the ten tribes to scatter throughout their empire .... These Israelites disappear from history permanently; they are called 'the ten lost tribes of Israel.'"[42]

In 597 BC, ten thousand Jews were deported from Palestine and forced to relocate in Babylon. In 586 BC, Judah itself ceased to exist as an independent kingdom.[43]

In AD 70, the Jews of Palestine were forcibly disbursed throughout the Roman Empire.

In view of these repeated displacements of Jews from their homeland, it might be assumed that Abraham's descendants would have lost their ethnic identity—due to racial intermarriages and cultural assimilation among the Gentiles with whom they lived.

Furthermore, from the time of Queen Esther to the

days of Hitler, what other ethnic people have been so globally despised simply because of their ethnic identity?

Yet, after millenniums of repeated dispersions and global anti-Semitism, Jews have remained a distinct ethnic people. As such, the stage is set for the fulfillment of this portion of God's promise to Abraham.

2. The rebirth of a nation

God's oath to Abraham included this promise: "Your descendants will take possession of the cities of their enemies."[44]

But following their global dispersion, Jewish nationhood in Palestine was surely one of the most unlikely events in history. Here is why:

Following the massive extermination of Jews during the Second World War, the United Nations initially favored an independent Jewish nation in a portion of Palestine. But due to unanimous opposition from Palestine's surrounding Arab nations, many UN nations began to waver in their support of such a Jewish homeland.

Palestine was, at that time, a UN mandate governed by Britain, whose policy was to keep the peace in Palestine—doing so by preventing Palestinian Jews from receiving weapons. But that restriction was not applied to Arabs, who were able to accumulate massive weaponry for the purpose of driving Jews from the region. Jewish survival in Palestine seemed hopeless. Even less likely was the successful formation of a Jewish nation. But it happened!

History thus testifies to God's faithfulness to these

two promises he made to Abraham: (1) the survival of his descendants as a distinct people, and (2) a specific place on earth where they could live.

3. Global blessing through Abraham's descendants

In addition to a promised land and a preserved ethnic identity, God's oath to Abraham included this promise: "Through your offspring all nations on earth will be blessed."[45]

The Hebrew word translated "offspring" is a singular noun, not plural. It can refer to a collective group of individuals in which the group is viewed as one unit, or that word can refer to a single individual.

But the apostle Paul leaves no doubt about which of those is the intended meaning in this particular oath of God. Writing to the Gentiles, he noted that blessing for all nations would come through one individual descendant of Abraham: "Now the promises were made to Abraham and to his offspring. It does not say, 'And to offsprings,' referring to many, but referring to one 'And to your offspring,' who is Christ."[46]

One of the issues that drives the global mission of God is his commitment by maximum oath to bless people of every ethnic nation on earth, not with some kind of generic blessing, such as rain and sunshine, but with the specific blessing of salvation that would come through that one descendant of Abraham, Christ.

But thousands of years after God's oath to Abraham, many people-nations of the world still remain unreached by the blessing that comes through the Messiah. Some are in regions where proclamation of the Gospel is prohibited or where language barriers prevent people from an adequate understanding of the Gospel. The Southern Baptist International Mission Board has, for example, identified hundreds of ethnic peoples among whom there are no known followers of Christ. For reasons just stated, many are currently unable to hear or comprehend the Gospel. *They remain unblessed with the blessing that has been promised by divine oath.*

The complete fulfillment of that "all nations" portion of God's oath seems improbable if not impossible. But just as God, in spectacular ways, fulfilled his promise of a Jewish nation with its own Palestinian homeland, we can be sure that he will also fulfill his promise of salvation's blessing ultimately reaching every ethnic nation on earth. Scripture, in fact, testifies that it will indeed happen.[47]

Since God's oath to Abraham is of such importance in scripture, we do well to examine all that is required for its fulfillment.

The Word "Nations"

Notice that God's blessing is promised to "all nations." In modern English, the word *nations* generally refers to geopolitical nations, also called countries. But in the Bible, the term refers to ethnic nations—any people group identified by its unique language and/or culture.

This is true in the Hebrew language of the Old Testament. For example, when God promised Israel, "I will drive out nations before you,"[48] he was referring to ethnic nations living in Canaan at that time: Hittites,

Amorites, Moabites, Girgashites, and Jebusites, among others.

The same is true in the New Testament, where the word *nations* is a translation of the Greek word *ethne*, from which we have our English word *ethnic*. It is clear, therefore, that when God promised to bless all nations on earth with the blessing of salvation, he was referring to ethnic nations.

This fact is of great importance as we consider Christ's mandate to "go and make disciples of all nations."[49] If we understand that word *nations* to mean geopolitical nations, we can rightly conclude that Christ's mandate has already been accomplished—because it is safe to say there are now followers of Christ in every geopolitical nation on earth. It is only when we are aware that the term *nations* is referring to ethnic nations that we realize the degree to which the requirements of that mandate remain unaccomplished.

The Word "All"

To Abraham, God said, "Through your offspring all nations on earth will be blessed."[50] It is not surprising, therefore, that the mandate Christ gave to his followers is to "make disciples of all nations."[51]

It is true that the Bible sometimes uses that word *all* in an absolute sense and sometimes in a relative sense, meaning "relatively all." Scripture says, for example, "The whole Judean countryside and all the people of Jerusalem went out to him [John the Baptist]. Confessing their sins, they were baptized by him in the Jordan River."[52] But scripture also says the Pharisees did not receive John's baptism. This is an example of the word *all* being used in a relative sense rather than in an absolute sense.

So how do we know what Christ meant when he told his disciples to make disciples of all nations? Does that mean all—or mostly all—nations? Scripture answers that question elsewhere, where we read that there will one day be worshipers for Christ in "every tribe and language and people and nation."[53] That word *every* is more absolute than the word *all* and is even more explicitly defined by scripture's assurance that there will be worshipers for Christ even among minority groups that are distinguished solely by their unique languages. It couldn't be more explicit than that!

Thus, because of God's oath to Abraham, and because of Christ's global mandate to his followers, we know what the mission of God is about. It's a mission that will be accomplished when at last salvation has reached every ethnic nation. It's a mission that was on the heart of the psalmist when he prayed, "May God be gracious to us and bless us and make his face shine upon us, that your ways may be known on earth, your salvation among all nations ... all the peoples ... all the ends of the earth."[54]

Notice the nature of the psalmist's petition. It begins with three repetitions of the word *us*: "God be gracious to us ... bless us ... make his face shine upon us." But the psalmist didn't stop there. He wanted all people-nations on earth to experience the blessing of salvation.

If we love and obey the Lord, we must not be satisfied with his blessing in our lives. Our desire must be the blessing of salvation that reaches all nations on earth.

One of the most important truths we can know about God is that he is committed by oath—the most solemn oath he can take—to bless people from every ethnic nation on earth with the blessing of salvation. This is a core purpose that underlies the global mission of God.

CHAPTER 4

CHRIST'S INHERITANCE

Nothing matters more to God than the inheritance he has promised his Son. It is a rich inheritance—one that includes worshipers for Jesus in every ethnic nation on earth. Only when that global mission of God is fully accomplished will Christ's inheritance be complete.

Inheritances are normally given—not earned. But Christ earned his inheritance. The importance of that inheritance can only be measured in terms of what it cost him. The cost was staggering. Hell has no greater horror than that which Christ experienced when "God made him who had no sin to be sin for us"[1] and "He personally carried away our sins in his own body on the cross."[2]

The late Dennis Kinlaw related a story that graphically pictures what happened when "the Lord laid on him [Christ] the iniquity of us all."[3] The story is about a daring medical experiment in which a young boy's life was saved. The boy had been diagnosed with a serious kidney infection, resulting in his kidneys being unable to cleanse his blood. His parents were told that he would die unless some radical procedure could be found to save him.

Numerous doctors consulted as they determined what might be done. It was decided that if the boy's blood system was connected to someone with healthy kidneys, perhaps the donor's kidneys would cleanse the boy's blood, allowing his diseased kidneys to recover. The doctors advised the boy's parents that this procedure had never been tried and would be an experiment with no assured outcome. But the parents quickly gave their consent to this attempt to save their son's life.

The blood type of the boy's father was the same as his son's, and the father quickly agreed to be the donor. He was taken to the hospital's operating room and placed on a bed alongside his son. The two blood systems were connected. As expected, when the boy's blood began streaming into the father and the father's blood began streaming into his son, the father's temperature began rising, and the boy's temperature began dropping. Eventually, both temperatures became normal.

The experiment appeared to be successful. After several days of maintaining a normal temperature, the son was released from the hospital. But although the father's temperature was normal, he was kept for additional observation. Two days later, his temperature skyrocketed, and he died.[4]

What an illustration of the amazing transfusion that took place when "God made him [Jesus] who had no sin to be sin for us, so that in him we might become the righteousness of God."[5] He became sin, and sinners became righteous, resulting in death for him and eternal life for sinners.

The price Jesus paid for his inheritance is best measured in terms of the anguish of his soul, not his body. Nevertheless, we do well not to discount his physical suffering, which was astonishing. It included a Roman scourging.

Typical of a Roman scourging, Christ would have been stripped of his clothes, with his body bent forward across a low pillar, so that his back was stretched and exposed to blows.

The Romans used short-handled whips, each containing several leather lashes. To each lash were attached pieces of lead and sharp bone fragments or metal. The strokes were laid on with full force. The effect was horrible. The skin and flesh of a person's back were gashed to the bone, and the victim's back became a mass of torn flesh.

Small wonder, says one commentator, that men not infrequently died as a result of this torture. It may be the best explanation for why Jesus died in such a relatively short time on the cross.

But before Christ went to the cross, his face had been brutalized—beaten repeatedly by the fists of religious leaders and Roman soldiers, both of whom also spit in his face. Hair was plucked from his beard, leaving his face bloodied from his torn beard and the crown of thorns that had been beaten down on his head.

Perhaps you have seen artistic drawings of Christ hanging from the cross. I have never seen a drawing that accurately portrayed Christ's face. It was swollen and deeply bruised from those repeated beatings—torn, swollen, bloodied, and spit covered. This is the condition in which Christ was led to the cross. Isaiah prophesied about Christ's face, saying, "His appearance was so disfigured beyond that of any man and his form marred beyond human likeness."[6]

It is no wonder that artists don't accurately draw a representation of Christ's face as he hung from the cross. It was gut-wrenchingly horrible.

Christ died not only from loss of blood but from suffocation. Years ago, there was an article in the prestigious *Journal of the American Medical Association*[7] describing death imposed by crucifixion. It noted that with a victim's full weight hanging from the arms, the chest was held in extended position, making it impossible for him to exhale, and therefore impossible to inhale. For that reason, it took effort for a victim to breathe, requiring him repeatedly to push himself up with his legs, holding that position just long enough to exhale and inhale.

That explains why all of Christ's statements from the cross are brief. He was struggling to breathe and lacked lung air for longer statements. That also explains why, when soldiers wanted to hasten the death of the three men hanging from the crosses, finding Jesus already dead but the two thieves still alive, they broke the thieves' legs. Now it would be impossible for them to push themselves up, and they would soon die from suffocation.

Throughout eternity, there will be a visible reminder of what Christ paid for his inheritance. Those nail scars were visible in his resurrected body[8] and will remain visible in his eternal, glorified body—a body in which he will appear as one who has been slain.[9] It is this visible reminder of Christ's sacrifice that will forever inflame the love and worship of those who were redeemed at the cost of his blood.

But Christ's physical suffering, horrendous though it was, paled in significance compared to the suffering of his soul. Scripture describes that suffering, saying Christ "endured the cross."[10] Consider what he endured: "The Lord has laid on him the iniquity of us all."[11] And "He [Christ] is the atoning sacrifice ... for the sins of the whole world."[12]

The guilt of all human sin ever committed was attributed to Jesus as he hung from the cross. It was in that sin-laden condition that he experienced the devastating anguish of separation from the first love of his life—his Father. "He who had lived wholly for the Father experienced full alienation from God .... His cry [at the cross] expresses the profound horror of separation from God .... The cry of dereliction expressed the unfathomable pain of real abandonment by the Father."[13]

Most astonishing is the fact that Christ became sin. "God made him who had no sin to be sin for us."[14] Sin was not like an external garment for Christ. It's what he became—sin personified! And as such, he also became a curse. "Christ redeemed us from the curse of the law by becoming a curse for us."[15]

Thus, the sinless one was made sin, came under sin's curse, and received sin's mandated death penalty. He who spoke often about the perfect union between himself and his Father now faced both the curse and the death penalty—at his Father's hands! "It was the LORD's will to crush him and cause him to suffer."[16] It was God himself who made Jesus an offering for sin, thereby crushing him.

Christ's heartbreak is seen most extensively in Gethsemane, where he was praying with his disciples prior to his arrest by Roman soldiers. His Gethsemane experience is described in the Gospels of Matthew, Mark, and Luke. Here is a compilation of those texts:

> Then Jesus went with his disciples to a place called Gethsemane, and he said to his disciples, "Sit here while I go over there and pray." He took with him Peter, James and John, and began to be deeply distressed and troubled. Then he said to them, "My soul is overwhelmed with sorrow to the point of death."
>
> Then he said, "Stay here and keep watch with me." Going a little farther, he fell on his face to the ground and prayed, "Abba, Father, all things are possible with you. If it is possible, may this cup be taken from me. Nevertheless, not my will, but yours be done."
>
> And when he came back [to his disciples] and found them sleeping from sorrow, he said to them, "Why are you sleeping? Rise and pray that you may not enter into temptation."
>
> Once more he went away and prayed the same thing. And there appeared to him an angel from heaven, strengthening

him. And being in an agony he prayed more fervently; and his sweat fell to the ground like drops of blood.

And when he came back [to his disciples] he again found them sleeping, because their eyes were heavy. So he left them and went away once more and prayed the third time, saying the same thing.[17]

Consider four statements in this text:

Notice Christ's posture as he prayed. The Gospel of Luke says Christ kneeled as he prayed. The Gospels of Matthew and Mark say he fell on his face on the ground. It appears that in his early praying, he was kneeling, but as his anguish became even more intense, he no longer knelt but fell prostrate on the ground. How unlike him! Elsewhere in scripture, we find him praying with his eyes facing heaven.[18] But in Gethsemane, he is face down on the ground. What a display of his extreme anguish!

Notice also that an angel came from heaven to strengthen him. Only one other time in Christ's earthly ministry did an angel intervene in his life. It was after he had fasted forty days and nights in the wilderness and was reduced to a skeleton—mere skin and bones. Without doubt, he was near death. On that occasion, God sent angels to minister to him, to save him from dying before he had accomplished the mission God had given him.

Now, here in Gethsemane, he was again near death, this time not from starvation but from sorrow. He described his life-threatening sorrow in these words: "My

soul is overwhelmed with sorrow to the point of death."[19]
His sorrow was nearly killing him. But he had not yet
finished the work God had given him to do. So once
again, God sent an angel to strengthen him.

Next, consider the nature of his perspiration. Scripture
says his sweat was blood-like as it fell to the ground. There
is a medical condition called "hematidrosis." Wikipedia
defines that term as follows:

> Hematidrosis, also called blood sweat, is a
> very rare condition in which a human sweats
> blood. [It] is a condition in which capillary
> blood vessels that feed sweat glands rupture
> causing them to exude blood, occurring
> under conditions of extreme physical or
> emotional stress. Dermatological research
> notes the presence of hematidrosis in people
> awaiting execution. It has been proposed
> as a possible explanation for Jesus' agony in
> the garden of Gethsemane.

Blood-mingled sweat. Extremely rare. It gives us
further insight into the intensity of Christ's anguish as he
prayed in Gethsemane.

Notice also Christ's use of the word *Abba* as he prayed.
It is an Aramaic word, which was the common language
in Palestine in Christ's day. *Vine's Expository Dictionary*
says, "Abba is the word framed by the lips of infants." It
was phonetically easy for a young child to pronounce,
similar to our English words *daddy* or *papa*.

It is also a word that was sometimes cried out loudly,

indicating intensity. The Bible says, "You have received the Spirit of adoption as sons, by whom we cry, 'Abba! Father!'"[20] And again, "God has sent the Spirit of his Son into our hearts, crying, 'Abba! Father!'"[21]

Referring to Christ's praying in Gethsemane, scripture says he prayed "with loud cries and tears."[22] Loud crying? Tears? Yes. Not all such crying is the same. Some may be reflective of disappointment or anger or physical pain. But Christ's crying in Gethsemane emanated from heartbreak.

In summary, Christ prayed face down on the ground, perspiring heavily with blood-mingled perspiration, while crying loudly to his Father with a cry typical of a young child: "Abba, Father, all things are possible for you. Remove this cup from me. Yet not what I will, but what you will."[23]

We most often think of what Christ's inheritance cost him, but that inheritance was costly for his Father as well. It required the blood sacrifice of his dearly loved Son. The cost to his Father is stated succinctly in these words: "God so loved the world that he gave his one and only Son."[24]

God's love for the world was not some sentimental feeling. It was costly. "God gave what was most dear to Him."[25]

Two thousand years earlier, God had pictured for us what it means for a father to sacrifice his one and only son. It's the account of Abraham offering his son, Isaac. There is a great deal of intended similarity between what Abraham did and what God did: (1) Both offerings were made at the same location—a hill in the land of Moriah, the same place later called Golgotha. (2) Both offerings involved a father's sacrifice of his dearly loved and only son. (3) In both offerings, each son submitted to the will of his father. (4) Both fathers offered their sons in confidence that their sons would be restored to life.

But there is a major difference between Abraham's sacrifice and God's sacrifice. Abraham's son was spared death, but God "did not spare his own Son, but gave him up for us all."[26]

The importance of Christ's inheritance is measured in part by the staggering price his Father paid for it. Jesus will ultimately receive his promised inheritance but only at the cost of his Father's extreme anguish—a sacrifice that can only be measured in light of the Father's great love for his Son. Consider what scripture says about that love:

Christ delighted in his Father's love and spoke of it repeatedly: "The Father loves the Son"[27] and "I have kept my Father's commands and remain in his love."[28]

To his disciples, Christ said, "As the Father has loved me, so have I loved you."[29]

In Christ's prayer for his disciples, he said to his Father, "You sent me and have loved them [those you have given me] even as you have loved me."[30] "You loved me before the creation of the world."[31] "I ... will continue to make you known in order that the love you have for me may be in them."[32]

John the Baptist also testified of the Father's love for his Son: "The Father loves the Son and has placed everything in his hands."[33]

In addition to these testimonies, God himself declared his love for his Son. At Christ's baptism, a voice from heaven announced, "This is my Son, whom I love; with him I am well pleased."[34]

Consider the pain that must have seared the heart of God upon hearing the cries of his Son, first in Gethsemane and then again at the cross. In Gethsemane, although remaining submissive to his Father's will, Christ pled to be saved—if possible—from the horror facing him. Again, at the cross, the Father witnessed the heartbreak of his Son as Jesus cried out, "My God, my God, why have you forsaken me?"[35]

The horror of Christ's alienation from his Father must be viewed in light of the intimate relationship that had always existed between them. Scripture graphically describes the intimacy of that relationship, saying Jesus had always lived "in the bosom of the Father."[36] (The significance of Christ's bosom-like relationship to his Father is discussed in chapter 2 under the heading "What Matters Most to Jesus.")

Christ delighted in his Father's love. Twice in his recorded prayer for his disciples, he referred to his Father's love for him.[37] Fifty-one times throughout his earthly ministry, Jesus referred to God as "My Father." It was a cherished Father-Son relationship to which Jesus testified, saying, "The Father loves the Son and shows him all he does."[38]

No love was ever so great as the mutual love that existed between the Father and his Son. It was because of that incomparable love relationship that the Father's curse of his Son was a nightmare of anguish for both of them. But that is the price they paid for Christ's inheritance. No wonder that inheritance is of such enormous importance to them both.

Thus far, we've been considering the staggering cost

of Christ's inheritance, both to the Father and his Son. But scripture reveals not only what Christ paid for his inheritance but also the reward he will receive as his inheritance. Never was an inheritance so costly, and never was an inheritance so glorious! Consider the following elements of the reward Christ has been promised.

Full Satisfaction

"When he [Christ] sees all that is accomplished by his anguish, he will be satisfied. And because of what he has experienced, my righteous servant will make it possible for many to be counted righteous."[39]

Notice how Christ will be satisfied. It will happen when he sees many counted righteous as a result of his anguish. How many? Scripture only says it will be "a great multitude that no one could count."[40] But although we don't know the size of that great multitude, scripture does specify from where those redeemed individuals will come: "from every tribe and language and people and nation."[41]

How wonderful—to him and to those who love him—is the assurance that Christ will one day see what his sacrificial death has accomplished: his complete satisfaction upon seeing that innumerable multitude of redeemed people, gathered from every ethnic nation on earth!

It is sobering to know that Christ's satisfaction awaits the fulfillment of his global mission. That fact ought to compel his lovers to be wholeheartedly committed to the completion of that mission.

Universal Jurisdiction and Allegiance

God has promised his Son an inheritance that includes Christ's global jurisdiction: "Ask me, and I will make the nations your inheritance, the ends of the earth your possession. You will rule them with an iron scepter; you will dash them to pieces like pottery."[42]

In addition to global jurisdiction, God has promised his Son the allegiance of all beings in existence. "At the name of Jesus every knee should bow, in heaven and on earth and under the earth."[43]

Bowing the knee to Jesus doesn't necessarily imply worship. It can be an act of fear or submission. Throughout history, for example, many knees have bowed to hated dictators. But of this we can be sure: bowing the knee implies allegiance, whether given voluntarily or by compulsion.

Allegiance to Jesus will be universal. There will be no exemptions for anyone, whether inhabitants of heaven, earth, or those "under the earth"—a term likely referring to those who have died. Even heaven itself has been placed under Christ's authority. "All authority in heaven and on earth has been given to me."[44]

Thus, Christ's inheritance will include the allegiance of all beings in existence, including the living and the dead, saints and sinners, angels and demons.

An Honorable Name

In Bible times, names were chosen because of their meaning, and scripture attaches great significance to the names of God, warning against using his name disrespectfully: "You shall not misuse the name of the LORD your God, for the LORD will not hold anyone guiltless who misuses his name."[45]

We speak of people who have "made a name for themselves." But Christ didn't make a name for himself. He was given a name. And what a name it was!

> God exalted him [Jesus] to the highest place and gave him the name that is above every name.[46]

> After he [Jesus] had provided purification for sins, he sat down at the right hand of the Majesty in heaven. So he became as much superior to the angels as the name he has inherited is superior to theirs.[47]

Christ had a God-given name even prior to his birth. In Bethlehem, an angel informed his mother that the child conceived in her womb was to be given the name "Jesus." That instruction was repeated to Joseph, Mary's husband. The angel explained to Joseph the significance of that name: "You are to give him the name Jesus, because he will save his people from their sins."[48]

The Greek word translated "Jesus" is a word meaning "Savior," "the One who saves." The salvation provided by Christ is the promise of deliverance from the greatest enslavement of all—the tyranny of sin.

Another name given to Jesus is "the Anointed One." It was a term used to describe Israel's kings. But Christ was not merely one among many kings. Twice the Bible calls him "King of kings and Lord of lords" or "Lord of lords and King of kings."[49]

The prophet Isaiah spoke of yet another name given to Jesus: "The virgin will be with child and will give birth to a son, and will call him Immanuel."[50] The Gospel of Matthew quotes this Isaiah text and adds the meaning of that Hebrew word *Immanuel*, saying it means "God with us."[51] What a declaration that is! It is not a great teacher who is with us. It is God himself! His name shouts the honor due him!

In the book of Revelation, we learn that at the summation of this age, Christ will be given an exalted name not yet known to us. It is a new name and a name "that no one knows but he himself."[52]

No other names in existence compare to the superiority of Christ's God-given names! Those names are an important part of Christ's inheritance.

An Indestructible Church

Some scriptures speak of the church as a local congregation of Christ's followers. But in some Bible texts, the term references the universal body of his followers. It is in the latter sense that Christ promised, "I will build my church, and the gates of hell shall not prevail against it."[53]

Christ's love for his church cost him dearly, but it ensured for him a treasured reward: "Christ loved the church and gave himself up for her to make her holy ... and to present her to himself as a radiant church, without stain or wrinkle or any other blemish."[54]

Christ referred to himself as the all-important

cornerstone on which that spiritual church is built. "The stone that the builders rejected has become the cornerstone."[55]

The apostle Paul wrote to Christians at Ephesus, saying they were built on a foundation with "Christ Jesus himself as the chief cornerstone."[56]

For those of us who are unfamiliar with the function of cornerstones, Wikipedia provides this description: "The cornerstone is the first stone set in the construction of a masonry foundation. All other stones will be set in reference to this stone, thus determining the position of the entire structure."

Throughout history, hell has been bent on the destruction of the church, but it has remained indestructible because Christ himself is the church's cornerstone. Using a different figure of speech, when referring to the church as the body of Christ, Christ is called "the head of the church."[57]

In summary, the church is an indestructible and radiant gift that Christ will one day present to himself as a part of the inheritance for which he "gave himself up."

Sovereign Ownership of Everything in Existence

Notice in the following Bible text the words *all things*: "[God's] Son, whom he appointed heir of all things."[58] The New Living Translation spells out what that term *heir* signifies: "God promised everything to the Son as an inheritance."[59]

Christ testified that his Father has given him

ownership of the entire universe. He said, "All things have been handed over to me by my Father."[60] Again, Christ said, "The Father loves the Son and has placed everything in his hands."[61]

The Creator of all things—that is, Jesus—has been given ownership of all things. They are his by right of creation. "For by him all things were created, in heaven and on earth, visible and invisible—all things were created through him and for him."[62]

But Christ is also owner of all things by right of inheritance. Scripture tells us that God has appointed his Son to be "heir of all things."[63]

Christ's inheritance includes his rightful ownership of the universe and everything in it. They are his by right of creation. And they are his by right of inheritance—an inheritance that is already his judicially and will be fully realized when even those who despise him must one day bow in submission at his feet, acknowledging his Lordship.

Eternal Joy for Jesus

Isaiah described Messiah as "a man of sorrows, and acquainted with grief."[64] Yet Christ spoke of his joy. To his disciples, he said, "These things I have spoken to you, that my joy may be in you, and that your joy may be full."[65]

Christ's joy was not due to the absence of sorrow. His joy was derived from accomplishing the will of his Father—because he knew what awaited him beyond the agony of the cross. "He was willing to die a shameful death on the cross because of the joy he knew would be his afterward. Now he is seated in the place of highest honor beside God's throne in heaven."[66] Mission accomplished! A God-given task completed! And now the joy of unprecedented honor at God's right hand.

Christ's eternal joy is an important part of his blood-bought inheritance: a reward for the Lamb who was slain! It is a reward that includes full satisfaction, universal allegiance, a name superior to every other name, an indestructible church, ownership of everything in existence, and eternal joy.

What an inheritance! Never was an inheritance so costly, and never was an inheritance so glorious!

The Question

What does Christ's inheritance have to do with the mission he has given to his followers? The following story gives perspective on that question.

One of the greatest mission mobilizations in church history occurred when, in the early 1700s, the Moravians of Germany became passionately committed to sending missionaries to the world's unevangelized peoples. They "commenced a round-the-clock 'prayer watch' that continued nonstop for over a hundred years ... 65 years after commencement of that prayer vigil, the small Moravian community had sent 300 missionaries to the ends of the earth."[67] Here is what drove that missionary passion. They said, "May the Lamb that was slain receive the reward of His suffering!"[68]

Among other things, the mission of God is about giving to Jesus the inheritance he earned when he suffered sin's curse in our place. How glad we should be to have a part in bringing his inheritance to completion!

CHAPTER 5

COMPASSION OF GOD

Does God ever cry? The Bible answers that question: "As [Jesus] approached Jerusalem and saw the city, he wept over it."[1]

The Lord's compassion is one of his worship-worthy attributes and is foundational to an understanding of what motivates the global mission on which he has set his heart. Consider some of the many Bible contexts in which that compassion is revealed:

Compassion for Widows

Jesus went with his disciples to the village of Nain .... A funeral procession was coming out as he approached the village gate. The boy who had died was the only son of a widow.... When the Lord saw her, his heart overflowed with compassion. "Don't cry!" he said. Then he walked over to the coffin and touched it, and the bearers stopped. "Young man," he said, "get up." Then the dead boy sat up and began to talk to those around him! And Jesus gave him back to his mother.[2]

Christ often required faith on the part of those needing his healing touch—but not in this instance. "As an act of love and sympathy for that mourning mother, Jesus, without first requiring faith from her or anyone else, commanded the young man to return to life."[3]

Widows were exceptionally vulnerable in Bible times. Throughout the Old Testament, there are repeated instructions regarding care for widows, orphans, and strangers. During Christ's earthly ministry, he warned against Jewish teachers of the law who "devour widows' houses."[4]

Even while suffering the anguish of his crucifixion, Jesus had compassion on his widowed mother, giving his favored disciple, John, the responsibility of caring for her.[5]

The first-century church reflected Christ's compassion for widows, entrusting to Stephen and six others the responsibility of ensuring that no widows were being overlooked in daily distribution of food.[6]

Throughout his earthly ministry, Christ's compassion embraced people who, like widows, were often unable to meet their own needs.

Compassion for Jerusalem's Inhabitants

Jerusalem, Jerusalem, … how often I have longed to gather your children together, as a hen gathers her chicks under her wings, but you were not willing. Look, your house is left to you desolate.[7]

> As [Jesus] approached Jerusalem and saw
> the city, he wept over it and said .... The
> days will come upon you when your
> enemies will ... dash you to the ground,
> you and the children within your walls.[8]

Notice that Christ's compassion for Jerusalem was not for
the city itself but for "you and the children within your
walls"—inhabitants of the city, many of whom would
later become disillusioned with him. They wanted a king
who would deliver them from Roman oppression, and
he was not the king they wanted. Nevertheless, Christ
grieved over them, foreseeing their massive slaughter at
the hands of Roman soldiers.

How remarkable that Christ's compassion was
extended even to people who would soon be joining their
religious leaders in demanding his crucifixion!

Compassion for Grieving Sisters

Scripture records three occasions when Christ wept. As
has been noted, he wept over Jerusalem's inhabitants
because of their imminent destruction. He wept again
in Gethsemane as he faced the agony of his Father's
curse. He also wept along with those who were grieving
the death of Lazarus. On that occasion, "he was deeply
moved in spirit and troubled."[9] Some have interpreted this
text to indicate Christ's anger. But that is not what was
understood by those who saw him weeping. They said,
"See how [Jesus] loved [Lazarus]!"[10] They certainly didn't
see anger in Christ's tears—nor should we.

Scripture instructs us to "weep with those who weep."[11] Never is compassion more needed than at the death of a loved one. By weeping with those who were grieving the death of Lazarus, Christ revealed one of the most important truths we can know about God: "The Lord is gracious and compassionate."[12]

On this occasion, Christ's compassion was costly. Raising Lazarus from the dead was the straw that broke the camel's back, so to speak. "From that day on [the Pharisees and the entire Jewish Sanhedrin] plotted to take [Christ's] life."[13]

Christ's compassion was on full display as he joined those who, with tears, were mourning the death of Lazarus.

Compassion for the Sick

Following the murder of John the Baptist, Christ "withdrew by boat privately to a solitary place," apparently seeking a period of aloneness. But the crowds followed him, and "he had compassion on them and healed their sick."[14]

Could there be no privacy for Christ? Must he always give himself to meeting endless human needs? Yes! Everywhere he went, there were sick people in need of his healing touch, and his compassion compelled him to meet those needs. On only one occasion—and entirely for the sake of his disciples—he led them to a place where they could be free of the demands of needy people. He said to his disciples, "Come away by yourselves to a desolate place and rest awhile."[15] Someone commented on that text, saying Christ wanted them to come apart and rest a while because otherwise they would physically "come apart."

How praiseworthy was Christ's compassion, taking into account not only needs of the sick but also the physical need of his weary disciples.

Compassion for the Blind and Lame

As Christ was en route to Jerusalem, he said to his disciples,

> We are going up to Jerusalem, and the Son of Man will be betrayed to the chief priests and the teachers of the law. They will condemn him to death and will turn him over to the Gentiles to be mocked and flogged and crucified.[16]

But even as Christ was nearing Jerusalem and facing the extreme horror of his crucifixion, his compassion prevailed when he saw human need:

> Two blind men were sitting by the roadside, and when they heard that Jesus was going by, they shouted, "Lord, Son of David, have mercy on us!" The crowd rebuked them and told them to be quiet, but they shouted all the louder, "Lord, Son of David, have mercy on us!" Jesus stopped and called them. "What do you want me to do for you?" he asked. "Lord," they answered, "we want our sight." Jesus

had compassion on them and touched
their eyes. Immediately they received
their sight and followed him.[17]

No one in that crowd expected Christ to do what
he did. From their perspective, this was a triumphant
occasion when Christ would deliver them from Roman
oppression. But amid all that adulation, his compassion
caused him to stop the entire crowd for the sake of two
blind men.

Later, upon Christ's arrival in Jerusalem at the temple,
he found merchants desecrating that place of worship. He
was furious and drove them out of the temple. But even in
that environment, "the blind and the lame came to him
at the temple, and he healed them."[18]

How extraordinary that Christ's compassion prevailed
even as he neared his own crucifixion!

Compassion for Sheeplike People

Jesus went through all the towns and
villages, teaching in their synagogues,
preaching the good news of the kingdom
and healing every disease and sickness.
When he saw the crowds, he had
compassion on them, because they were
harassed and helpless, like sheep without
a shepherd.[19]

The twenty-third psalm is the most memorized and most
quoted text in the Bible. And for good reason. It begins

with the psalm writer's declaration, "The Lord is my shepherd," and then proceeds to detail the benefits of that shepherd-sheep relationship: "he leads me ... he restores my soul. He guides me."[20]

Finally, the psalmist stops testifying about the Lord and begins speaking directly to him:

> I will not be afraid, for you are close beside me. Your rod and your staff protect and comfort me. You prepare a feast for me in the presence of my enemies. You welcome me as a guest, anointing my head with oil. My cup overflows with blessings. Surely your goodness and unfailing love will pursue me all the days of my life. [21]

We may not appreciate being compared to sheep. They are not the smartest or most self-sufficient animals. Volumes have been written about sheep and their need of human care. Some of my growing-up years were spent on a farm. Among other animals, we had sheep. I learned that they are pitiful creatures without human caregivers—defenseless and unable to run fast enough to escape deadly pursuers. But the psalmist delighted in being among the Lord's sheep, saying, "We are his people, the sheep of his pasture."[22]

How worship worthy is the one whose compassion is compared to a shepherd's care of his totally dependent sheep!

Compassion for Children

Jesus held children on his lap—much to the consternation of those who thought he could make better use of his time. But by so doing, he was reflecting an important truth: children have a special place in the heart of God.

That truth was amply demonstrated in the days of Jonah, a prophet who had lost touch with the heart of God. He wanted the wicked city of Nineveh destroyed—never mind the fact that tens of thousands of young children would be included in that destruction. The Lord rebuked Jonah, saying, "Should I not have compassion on Nineveh, the great city in which there are more than 120,000 persons who do not know the difference between their right and left hand?"[23] The Hebrew word translated "compassion" can also be translated "pity" or "mercy."[24]

With reference to the population of Nineveh, one well-respected commentary states, "Not to be able to distinguish between the right and left hand is a sign of mental infancy. This is not to be restricted, however, to the very earliest years ... but must be extended to the age of seven years, in which children first learn to distinguish between right and left .... Children who cannot distinguish between right and left, cannot distinguish good from evil, and are not yet accountable."[25]

But Jonah wasn't concerned about those not-yet-accountable children. He wanted divine destruction of the entire population. But God's compassion prevailed over Jonah's strong objection—compassion particularly on children, while also giving even the wicked adult population of the city an opportunity to avoid destruction.

The result? The largest spiritual awakening in recorded history.

Children prompted the compassion of God, even when their parents were wicked!

Compassion for God's Imperfect Followers

One of the chief evidences of God's compassion is the extreme grace he extends to those who follow him imperfectly. In testimony of that truth, the Bible doesn't hide the imperfections of many of history's spiritual heroes.

Noah got drunk and slept in the nude, enabling Canaan, one of his sons, to disgrace him. Yet scripture says, "Noah found favor in the eyes of the Lord …. and he walked with God."[26]

Job's faith in the Lord remained strong throughout much of his life. But his circumstances finally overwhelmed his trust in God, and he began to protest the suffering God was allowing in his life. How did God respond to Job's loss of trust? First with a gentle rebuke, but then with unprecedented blessing: "The Lord made [Job] prosperous again and gave him twice as much as he had before …. The Lord blessed the latter part of Job's life more than the first."[27] Thus, even when Job's faith faltered, God's compassion toward him remained steadfast.

Abraham didn't wait for God to fulfill his promise of a son to be born through Abraham's wife, Sarah. He gave up on God and had a son by Sarah's servant, Hagar, whose descendants became enemies of Israel. Yet Abraham was called a friend of God.[28]

Jacob deceived his father in order to steal the birthright that rightly belonged to his older brother, Esau. Yet scripture affirms that God loved Jacob.[29]

Moses committed murder in Egypt and later, in a fit of anger, disobeyed the Lord and was therefore disqualified from entering Canaan, the Promised Land. Yet when Miriam and Aaron attempted to replace Moses as leaders of Israel, God rebuked them, saying, "When a prophet of the LORD is among you, I reveal myself to him in visions, I speak to him in dreams. But this is not true of my servant Moses; he is faithful in all my house. With him I speak face to face ... he sees the form of the LORD."[30]

From his birth, Samson was designated by God as the one who would begin delivering Israel from Philistine bondage.[31] But you would be hard-pressed to find in scripture any less perfect example of a servant of the Lord. Repeatedly, nevertheless, "the Spirit of the Lord came upon him in power."[32] And in Hebrews 11:32, he is included among those "who through faith conquered kingdoms."

Elijah, when he knew that wicked Queen Jezebel intended to kill him, "was afraid and ran for his life ... and prayed that he might die."[33] Yet, when Christ took Peter, James, and John to a high mountain and revealed to them his transfigured glory, "there appeared before them Moses and Elijah, talking with Jesus."[34] Elijah did not trust God to protect him from Jezebel, but he was ranked with Moses as one of the spiritual giants in Israel's history.

King David committed adultery and then murder— for the sake of stealing Uriah's wife. One might assume that such flagrant disobedience to the moral law of God would bring an end to God's blessing in David's life. God did, in fact, discipline David, but in God's economy, discipline is not rejection. As scripture puts it, "The Lord disciplines those he loves."[35] Despite his moral failure, "[God] testified concerning [David]: 'I have found David son of Jesse a man after my own heart; he will do everything I want him to do.'"[36] David's failure notwithstanding, God did not rescind his promise to give him a son (Messiah) who would reign over the nations forever.

John the Baptist, when imprisoned by King Herod, became doubtful about whether Christ was in fact the promised Messiah. But notice what Jesus said about John: "Among those born of women there is no one greater than John."[37] Although Christ modified that statement by saying that even those who are least in the kingdom of God are greater than John, Jesus obviously held John in high esteem—despite his faltering faith as he remained imprisoned at the hands of a wicked king.

None of Christ's disciples failed him more miserably than Peter did when Christ was nearing his crucifixion. To save himself from harm, Peter repeatedly claimed that he didn't even know Christ. One might think such denial would disqualify him from any future ministry in the emerging church. But no, Christ entrusted to him a lifetime of fruitful ministry, beginning with the salvation of three thousand people in response to Peter's preaching on the day of Pentecost.[38]

The apostle Paul and Barnabas had been companions in the first evangelistic campaign ever to occur in Asia

Minor. But when a second campaign was planned, "Barnabas wanted to take John, also called Mark, with them, but Paul did not think it wise to take him …. They had such a sharp disagreement that they parted company."[39] Did that tension between them disqualify them for any useful service in Christian ministry? Apparently not, because the apostle Paul and Barnabas both continued in separate ministries.

The apostle Paul acknowledged his imperfection. He said, "I don't mean to say … that I have already reached perfection! But I keep working toward that day when I will finally be all that Christ Jesus saved me for and wants me to be."[40] Keenly aware of his imperfections, Paul considered himself "less than the least of all God's people."[41] Yet he was singularly used of God to plant churches throughout the Mediterranean world and to write most of the books of the New Testament.

I heard a mission leader make this statement: "God doesn't send any 'finished products' to the mission field— mainly because he doesn't have any to send!"

I heard someone else say, "If you think you have achieved sinless perfection, check with your spouse. He or she can correct your thinking."

All of these testimonials affirm this statement of King David, a testimony reflecting David's own life experience: "As a father has compassion on his children, so the LORD has compassion on those who fear him; for he knows how we are formed, he remembers that we are dust …. From everlasting to everlasting the LORD's love is with those who fear him."[42]

These are just some of many instances of God's

compassion toward individuals. We turn our attention now to God's compassion for an entire nation.

Compassion for a Nation

Abraham's descendants eventually became a divided nation, separated into a northern kingdom (Israel) and a southern kingdom (Judah). Never has there been any nation toward which God has shown compassion like that which he extended to Israel and Judah—even when both of them eventually turned their backs on him.

Isaiah wrote of God's irrevocable compassion toward Judah:

> For a brief moment I abandoned you, but with deep compassion I will bring you back. In a surge of anger I hid my face from you for a moment, but with everlasting kindness I will have compassion on you.[43]

> Can a mother forget the baby at her breast and have no compassion on the child she has borne? Though she may forget, I will not forget you! See, I have engraved you on the palms of my hands.[44]

This latter scripture text has special meaning for me. For years, I have often written on a palm of my hand some reminder of an approaching task I needed to accomplish. Every time I opened that hand, I saw that reminder, written with a ballpoint pen. But God's reminders aren't written with ink—easily washed off. This text says his reminders are engraved in his hands. That is permanent. And it is not in one hand but both hands!

Although this text is figurative speech (God doesn't have physical hands), its message is unmistakable: God's compassion on his ancient people is permanent.

Jeremiah affirmed God's compassion for both Judah and Israel. Of Judah, he said, "This I call to mind and therefore I have hope: Because of the LORD's great love we are not consumed, for his compassions never fail. They are new every morning."[45]

Of Ephraim (Israel), God said, "Is not Ephraim my dear son, the child in whom I delight? Though I often speak against him, I still remember him. Therefore my heart yearns for him; I have great compassion for him, declares the Lord."[46]

Hosea wrote of God's compassion toward Israel:

> When Israel was a child, I loved him, and out of Egypt I called my son. But the more I called Israel, the further they went from me …. How can I give you up, Ephraim? How can I hand you over, Israel? How can I treat you like Admah? How can I make you like Zeboiim? My heart is changed within me; all my compassion is aroused.[47]

Nehemiah marveled at God's compassion toward the people of Judah even when they, like their ancestors, were unfaithful to him: "You are a forgiving God, gracious and compassionate, slow to anger and abounding in love. Therefore you did not desert them [your people] even when they cast for themselves an image of a calf and said 'This is your god, who brought you up out of Egypt,' or when they committed awful blasphemies."[48]

Joel, writing to the people of Judah, assured them of God's welcome if they returned to him: "Return to the LORD your God, for he is gracious and compassionate, slow to anger and abounding in love."[49]

Can any truth be more reassuring than the irreversible and unconditional nature of God's compassion on people with whom he has made an everlasting covenant?

Compassion for the Condemned

The subject of what lies beyond the grave touches a sensitive nerve in the heart of virtually every human being. As scripture says, "He [God] has also set eternity in the hearts of men."[50] Even for people best described as irreligious, the topic of human mortality keeps demanding attention. The death of friends and loved ones serve as repeated reminders of this sobering topic. It is, therefore, a topic of universal interest, even in societies where secularism is making religion seem irrelevant. It is significant that the Bible, from beginning to end, addresses this all-important topic.

In large part, the mission of God is driven by his compassion for people who are under condemnation: "This is the judgement, that the Light has come into the world, and men loved the darkness rather than the Light, for their deeds were evil."[51]

As my mother-in-law was nearing the end of her earthly journey, she said to us, "Now, children, don't begrudge me my glory day"! And glory day it is for those who are followers of Jesus. But it is a day of indescribable horror for those who have not put their trust in him.

But that is a topic no one wants to hear about, talk about, or even think about. Modern Christendom for the most part refuses to proclaim the fate of unrepentant sinners. It can, after all, be awkward to defend Christ's descriptions of hell when unbelievers ridicule the concept of a God who would inflict such horror on people. When was the last time you heard a sermon on hell? After more than seventy years of church attendance, I have never heard such a sermon.

But we cannot ignore this unpleasant topic if we are to understand and share God's compassion for those who, in their unrepentance, are under divine condemnation.

Compassion, by its nature, requires an awareness of need. The greater the perceived need, the greater the potential for compassion.

No need can ever be greater than the need of sinners who die in unrepentance. They will perish.[52] But scripture assures us that God is "not wanting anyone to perish."[53] His compassion is best measured in terms of what it cost him to make it possible for sinners to avoid perishing:

> God so loved the world that he gave his
> one and only Son, that whoever believes
> in him shall not perish.[54]

God did not send his Son into the world
to condemn the world, but to save the
world through him.[55]

God our Savior ... wants all men to be
saved.[56]

Heaven is more wonderful than the human mind can
imagine. "No eye has seen, no ear has heard, no mind
has conceived what God has prepared for those who love
him."[57]

Hell, likewise, is more horrifying than any human
mind can image. Jonathan Edwards, a theologian of
years gone by, preached a sermon titled "Sinners in
the Hands of an Angry God." Church historians are in
wide agreement that the preaching of this sermon was
the catalyst for the first great spiritual awakening in
North America.[58]

John the Baptist pled with people to "flee from the
wrath to come."[59] But how can people flee danger of
which they are unaware? In a conversation I had with
Bible scholar Dr. Larry Dixon,[60] he noted that Christ
spoke more extensively about hell than about heaven.
Why would he do that? For the same reason a loving
parent warns a child repeatedly about some potential
danger.

My wife and I, with our two young children,
lived several years in a remote interior region of Papua
New Guinea. We had two appliances in our kitchen: a
woodstove and a small refrigerator. Occasionally, the stove
became overheated, turning cherry red near the firebox.

About which of those two appliances do you think we spoke most frequently to our children? We repeatedly warned them not to get near that stove.

Similarly, it was in compassion that Christ repeatedly warned about the eternity that awaits unrepentant people. He described explicitly the horrors of hell. He depicted it as a place of "weeping and gnashing of teeth."[61] Gnashing of teeth has been interpreted by some as an indication of anger. But most often in scripture, such gnashing of teeth is accompanied by weeping. It is therefore more likely an indication of enormous pain.

But if the weeping is due to pain, what might be the nature of such pain? Is it due to a sense of hopelessness and despair? Is it due to tormenting remembrances of what brought you to this place? Is it due to the realization that all of this could have been avoided? Is it due to the awareness that loved ones are sharing the same fate? Or is the weeping due to a combination of some or all of the above?

I have experienced heartbreak that caused me to weep hard several times a day, day after day—until finally I was too emotionally exhausted to continue weeping. But I have never experienced a circumstance in which everyone, myself included, was weeping endlessly and uncontrollably—a whole room filled with the sound of continuous crying. One of the most dreadful features of hell is that all its occupants are weeping.

It appears that inhabitants of hell experience pain. Twice Christ called hell "the fiery furnace."[62] On two other occasions, he called it a place of "eternal fire."[63] He also called it a place of "unquenchable fire."[64] In his parable of the rich man and Lazarus, Christ quoted the rich man saying, "I am in agony in this fire."[65] It is hard to imagine any pain greater than that inflicted by fire. No wonder it causes gnashing of teeth.

Christ further described hell as a place of "outer darkness."[66] The apostle Jude described it as a place of "blackest darkness."[67] Hell is a place of intense darkness.

In most darkness, there are at least some particles of light called photons. Night vision goggles can amplify those particles, enabling people to see what otherwise would be invisible to them. But in hell, there will be no particles of light. It is as Jude 13 describes it. It is darkness in the most absolute degree.

Some have taken comfort in the belief that even if they end up in hell, they will be in the company of many of their friends. But the darkness will separate every person from visual contact with anyone else. Each person will be isolated in their own solitary confinement, able only to hear the weeping and wailing of those in torment all around them.

With the exception of the death sentence, "life without parole" is the severest sentence we impose on criminals. But hell is not life without parole. It is eternity without parole. The greatest single horror of hell is this: after ten thousand years, its inhabitants have not shortened their anguish in the slightest.

No wonder scripture says, "It is a fearful thing to fall into the hands of the living God."[68] No wonder we don't hear sermons about the eternity that awaits unrepentant sinners! And no wonder some have attempted to de-horrify what the Bible says on that subject.

The term *gospel* means "good news." And indeed, never was news half so good as that which describes the eternity that awaits sinners who have put their trust in Christ. But never was news more horrific than that which describes the eternity that awaits those still under condemnation for their sin. It is that awful horror that prompts the compassion of God.

Wonder above all other wonders is God's compassion for people worthy of condemnation. *Never was compassion so costly,* requiring the sacrifice of his sinless Son. Importantly, it is compassion that will be fully satisfied only when the global mission of God is accomplished and sinners from every ethnic nation have been rescued from a horrible eternity.

We do well to share this compassion of God, engaging fully and sacrificially with him as he pursues the completion of his global mission.

One of the greatest mission mobilizations in church history was prompted, in part, by God's compassion for people in danger of perishing. It occurred when, in the early 1700s, the Moravians of Germany became passionately committed to sending missionaries to the world's unevangelized peoples. They "commenced a round-the-clock 'prayer watch' that continued nonstop for over a hundred years .... 65 years after commencement of that prayer vigil, the small Moravian community had sent 300 missionaries to the ends of the earth."[69]

But there was a second factor that contributed to the Moravians' missionary passion. They said, "May the Lamb that was slain receive the reward of His suffering!"[70]

Compassion for those in danger of perishing eternally, and passion to see Jesus receive what he earned when he went to the cross on behalf of condemned sinners. May we be motivated by these same two passions!

NOTES

Preface

1   Philippians 2:8 (ESV).
2   Luke 12:50 (NIV).
3   Luke 12:50 (NASB).
4   Luke 12:50 (NLT).
5   Isaiah 62:5 (NIV).
6   Isaiah 55:8–9 (ESV).
7   Romans 11:34 (ESV).
8   Romans 11:33 (ESV).
9   Jeremiah 33:3 (NIV).
10 Job 26:14 (NASB).

Chapter 1

1   Genesis 3:8 (ESV).
2   John 4:24 (NIV).
3   First Timothy 6:16 (NIV).
4   Exodus 33:20 (NIV).
5   Acts 9:5 (NIV).
6   First Timothy 6:16 (NIV).
7   Genesis 6:5–6 (ESV).
8   Genesis 6:6 (NLT).
9   Matthew 17:3 (NIV).
10 Exodus 33:11 (NIV).

11   Deuteronomy 5:4; 34:10 (NIV).

12   Numbers 12:6–8 (ESV).

13   Psalm 34:15 (NIV).

14   John 5:39–40 (NIV).

15   John 14:6 (NIV).

16   Second Corinthians 5:19 (NIV).

17   John 3:16 (NIV).

18   John 3:17 (NIV).

19   Genesis 12:3 (NIV).

20   Genesis 22:17–18 (NIV).

21   Genesis 26:4 (NIV).

22   Genesis 18:18 (NIV).

23   Genesis 26:4 (NIV).

24   Genesis 28:14 (NIV).

25   Galatians 3:16 (NIV).

26   Psalm 67:1–7 (NIV).

27   Acts 1:8 (NIV).

28   Matthew 28:19 (NIV).

29   First Kings 10:23–24 (NIV).

30   Proverbs 1:7; 9:10 (NIV).

31   Mark 16:15 (ESV).

32   Genesis 1:11, 12, 21, 24a, 24b, 25b (NIV).

33   Genesis 1:22, 28 (NIV).

34   Revelation 5:9; 7:9 (NIV).

35   Revelation 19:6–8 (NIV).

36   First John 2:2 (NIV).

37   Zephaniah 3:17 (NIV).

38   Isaiah 62:5 (NIV).

39   Revelation 5:9 (NIV).

40   James 2:23 (NIV).

41   Isaiah 41:8 (NIV).

42   Exodus 33:11 (NIV).

43   Numbers 12:2 (NIV).

44   Numbers 12:6–8 (NIV).

45   John 15:15 (NIV).

46   Luke 12:4 (NIV).

47 Catesby Paget.

48 Ephesians 2:6 (NIV).

49 Hebrews 12:2 (NIV).

50 Second Corinthians 5:8 (NIV).

51 Revelation 21:3 (NIV).

52 Hebrews 11:5 (NIV).

53 Genesis 5:24 (NIV).

54 Genesis 6:8 (NIV).

55 Genesis 6:9 (NIV).

56 Exodus 19:4–5 (NIV).

57 Joshua 1:5 (NIV).

58 First Kings 8:27 (NIV).

59 armstronginstitute.org Jerusalem's temples: the archeological evidence.

60 Exodus 29:42 (NIV).

61 Exodus 40:34; 2 Chronicles 7:2 (NIV).

62 First Kings 7:48 (NIV).

63 Matthew 1:23 (NIV).

64 Matthew 23:37 (NIV).

65 John 14:2–3 (NIV).

66 John 17:24 (NIV).

67 Luke 23:43 (NIV).

68 Hebrews 13:5 (ESV).

69 Matthew 28:20 (NIV).

70 Samuel Rutherford.

71 First Corinthians 1:9 (ESV).

72 First John 1:7 (NIV).

73 Alexander Ross, *The Epistles of James and John*, p. 143.

74 Luke 10:38–42 (NIV).

75 Revelation 3:20 (NIV).

76 Revelation 19:9 (NIV).

77 Revelation 19:6 (NIV).

78 Revelation 7:9 (NIV).

79 Matthew 6:9 (NIV).

80 Hebrews 2:10 (NIV).

81 Matthew 12:50 (NIV).

82 Romans 8:14, 19; Galatians 4:6; Philippians 2:15; 1 John 3:1–2 (NIV).

83 Romans 8:17 (NIV).

84 John 3:7 (NIV).

85 Romans 8:15; Galatians 4:6 (NIV).

86 First John 2:2 (NIV).

87 Genesis 12:3 (NIV).

88 Ephesians 5:32 (NIV).

89 John 14:17 (NIV).

90 John 15:4 (NIV).

91 John 17:21 (NIV).

92 First Corinthians 3:16 (NIV).

93 Second Corinthians 5:17 (ESV).

94 Colossians 1:27 (NIV).

95 First John 4:4 (NIV).

96 John 7:38–39 (NIV).

97 Matthew 16:18 (NIV).

98 Psalm 67:1–2 (NIV).

99 John 15:5 (ESV).

Chapter 2

1 Revelation 5:9 (NIV).

2 Mark 11:17 (NIV).

3 John 4:20 (NIV).

4 John 4:23 (NIV).

5 Brown, Driver, Briggs Hebrew-English Lexicon, p. 1005.

6 Psalm 95:6 (NIV).

7 Daniel 2:46 (NLT).

8 Daniel 3:4–5 (NIV).

9 Matthew 4:8–9 (NIV).

10 Job 1:20 (NIV).

11 Ephesians 5:19a (NIV).

12 Ephesians 5:19b (NIV).

13 Psalm 19:1 (NIV).

14 Isaiah 6:3 (NIV).

15   shutterstock.com/g/Space-kraft.

16   thoughtco.com.

17   education.jlab.org.

18   Romans 8:21 (NIV).

19   Johnson Oatman Jr., p. 425

20   Second Corinthians 3:18 (NIV).

21   Romans 8:28–29 (NIV).

22   John W. Peterson, *In the Image of God.*

23   Galatians 5:22–23 (NIV).

24   First John 3:2 (NIV).

25   Matthew 5:16 (NIV).

26   Second Corinthians 4:6 (ESV).

27   Colossians 2:9 (NIV).

28   Hebrews 1:3 (NIV).

29   John 14:9 (NIV).

30   John 11:5 (NIV).

31   John 11:4 (NIV).

32   John 11:40 (NIV).

33   John 21:18 (NIV).

34   John 21:19 (NIV).

35   John 9:2 (NIV).

36   John 9:3 (NIV).

37   John 9:38 (NIV).

38   Philippians 1:29 (ESV).

39   Philippians 1:20 (NIV).

40   Quoted in goodreads.com. https://www.goodreads.com/quotes/672075.

41   First Corinthians 10:31 (NIV).

42   John 15:5–8 (NIV).

43   John 12:27–28 (NIV).

44   Mark 15:34 (NIV).

45   John 1:18 (NASB).

46   Second Samuel 12:3 (NASB).

47   Isaiah 53:6 (NIV).

48   Galatians 3:13 (NIV).

49   Matthew 12:31–32 (NIV).

50 Philippians 2:9–11 (NIV).

51 John 5:22–23 (NIV).

52 John 17:24 (NIV).

53 Hebrews 1:6 (NIV).

54 Matthew 3:17 (NIV).

55 Matthew 17:5 (NIV).

56 Psalm 2:7 (NIV).

57 John 16:13–14 (NIV).

58 Acts 7:55–56 (NIV).

59 Acts 4:8–10 (NIV).

60 James McConkey, *Revival and the Holy Spirit.*

61 Psalm 8:1 (NIV).

62 Psalm 19:1 (NIV).

63 Psalm 24:9–10 (NIV).

64 Psalm 29:1–2 (NIV).

65 Psalm 57:5 (NIV).

66 Psalm 63:1, 3 (NIV).

67 Psalm 72:18–19 (NIV).

68 Psalm 79:9 (NIV).

69 Psalm 90:16 (NLT).

70 Psalm 96:1, 3 (NIV).

71 Psalm 96:7–8 (NIV).

72 Psalm 102:15 (NIV).

73 Psalm 104:31 (NIV).

74 Psalm 108:5 (NIV).

75 Psalm 113:4 (NIV).

76 Psalm 115:1 (NIV).

77 Psalm 138:4–5 (NIV).

78 Matthew 24:14 (NIV).

79 Mark 13:10 (NIV).

80 Revelation 12:12 (NIV).

81 Luke 4:5–7 (NIV).

82 Second Thessalonians 2:4 (NIV).

83 Isaiah 43:7 (NIV).

84 John 13:21–27 (NIV).

85 Romans 1:21, 25 (NIV).

86   Piper, *Let the Nations Be Glad!*

87   Adkins, *Glorify Thy Name.*

Chapter 3

1   Hebrews 6:18 (NIV).

2   Quoted on Facebook by Word International Ministries, Ontario, Canada.

3   Second Peter 1:4 (NIV).

4   Jeremiah 29:11 (NIV).

5   Isaiah 54:10 (NIV).

6   Isaiah 41:10 (NIV).

7   John 10:27–28 (NIV).

8   Psalm 32:8 (ESV).

9   Numbers 14:21–23 (NIV).

10   Jeremiah 22:24–25 (NIV).

11   Jeremiah 46:18, 24 (NIV).

12   Ezekiel 18:3–4 (NIV).

13   Romans 14:11 (NIV).

14   Genesis 12:2–3 (ESV).

15   Genesis 18:18 (NIV).

16   Genesis 22:18 (NIV).

17   Genesis 26:4 (NIV).

18   Genesis 28:13–14 (NIV).

19   Genesis 9:11 (NIV).

20   John Walvoord, Millennial Series. The Abrahamic Covenant and Premillennialism. Bible.org. (Genesis 17:3–7 (NIV)

21   Deuteronomy 29:2, 9 (NIV).

22   Second Samuel 23:5 (NIV).

23   Second Chronicles 7:17–18 (NIV).

24   Hebrews 9:15 (NIV).

25   Hebrews 7:22 (NIV).

26   Hebrews 9:26–28 (ESV).

27   Wikipedia, "Abrahamic Covenant," https://en.wikipedia.org/wiki/Covenant_(biblical).

28   Genesis 15:17 (NIV).

29 Exodus 3:2–6 (NIV).

30 Exodus 19:18 (NIV).

31 Exodus 13:21 (NIV).

32 Genesis 22:16, 18 (ESV).

33 Psalm 89:3–4 (NIV).

34 Deuteronomy 1:34–36 (NIV).

35 Amos 8:7–8 (ESV).

36 Ezekiel 16:8, 15, 59 (NIV).

37 Isaiah 62:8 (NIV).

38 Hebrews 7:20–21 (NIV).

39 Isaiah 45:23 (NIV).

40 Hebrews 6:13, 16, 18 (ESV).

41 Keil and Deilitzsh, *Commentaries on the Old Testament, The Pentateuch*, vol. 1, p. 250.

42 jewishvirtuallibrary.org.

43 jewishvirtuallibrary.org.

44 Genesis 22:17 (NIV).

45 Genesis 22:18 (NIV).

46 Galatians 3:16 (ESV).

47 Revelation 5:9 (NIV).

48 Exodus 34:24 (NIV).

49 Matthew 28:19 (NIV).

50 Genesis 22:18 (NIV).

51 Matthew 28:19 (NIV).

52 Mark 1:5 (NIV).

53 Revelation 5:9 (NIV).

54 Psalm 67:1–7 (NIV).

Chapter 4

1 Second Corinthians 5:21 (NIV).

2 First Peter 2:24 (ESV).

3 Isaiah 53:6 (NIV).

4 Kinlaw, 1984. "October 24," *This Day with the Master*.

5 Second Corinthians 5:21 (NIV).

6 Isaiah 52:14 (NIV).

7   Edwards et al., 1986

8   John 20:27 (NIV).

9   Revelation 5:6 (NIV).

10 Hebrews 12:2 (NIV).

11 Isaiah 53:6 (NIV).

12 First John 2:2 (NIV).

13 William Lane, *The Gospel According to Mark*, p. 573.

14 Second Corinthians 5:21 (NIV).

15 Galatians 3:13 (NIV).

16 Isaiah 53:10 (NIV).

17 Compiled from these Bible texts: Matthew 26:36–46; Mark 14:32–41; Luke 22:40–46.

18 John 11:41 (ESV).

19 Matthew 26:38 (NIV).

20 Romans 8:15 (ESV).

21 Galatians 4:6 (ESV).

22 Hebrews 5:7 (ESV).

23 Mark 14:36 (ESV).

24 John 3:16 (NIV).

25 Leon Morris, *The Gospel According to John*, p. 230.

26 Romans 8:32 (NIV).

27 John 5:20 (NIV).

28 John 15:10 (NIV).

29 John 15:9 (NIV).

30 John 17:23 (NIV).

31 John 17:24 (NIV).

32 John 17:26 (NIV).

33 John 3:35 (NIV).

34 Matthew 3:17 (NIV).

35 Matthew 27:46 (NIV).

36 John 1:18 (NASB).

37 John 17:23, 26 (NIV).

38 John 5:20 (NIV).

39 Isaiah 53:11 (NLT).

40 Revelation 7:9 (NIV).

41 Revelation 5:9 (NIV).

42 Psalm 2:8–9 (NIV).

43 Philippians 2:10 (NIV).

44 Matthew 28:18 (NIV).

45 Exodus 20:7 (NIV).

46 Philippians 2:9 (NIV).

47 Hebrews 1:3–4 (NIV).

48 Matthew 1:21 (NIV).

49 Revelation 19:16; 17:14 (NIV).

50 Isaiah 7:14 (NIV).

51 Matthew 1:23 (NIV).

52 Revelation 3:12; 19:12 (NIV).

53 Matthew 16:18 (ESV).

54 Ephesians 5:25–27 (NIV).

55 Mark 12:10 (ESV).

56 Ephesians 2:20 (NIV).

57 Ephesians 5:23 (ESV).

58 Hebrews 1:2 (NIV).

59 Hebrews 1:2 (NLT).

60 Matthew 11:27 (ESV).

61 John 3:35 (NIV).

62 Colossians 1:16 (ESV).

63 Hebrews 1:2 (NIV).

64 Isaiah 53:3 (ESV).

65 John 15:11 (ESV).

66 Hebrews 12:2 (NLT).

67 Christian History Institute.

68 Wikipedia. *Moravian slaves.*

Chapter 5

1 Luke 19:41 (NIV).

2 Luke 7:11–15 (NLT).

3 Norval Geldenhuys, *Commentary on the Gospel of Luke*, p. 223.

4 Mark 12:40; Luke 20:47 (NIV).

5 John 19:26–27 (NIV).

6 Acts 6:1–6 (NIV).

7   Matthew 23:37; Luke 13:34 (NIV).

8   Luke 19:41–44 (NIV).

9   John 11:33 (NIV).

10 John 11:36 (NIV).

11 Romans 12:15 (ESV).

12 Psalm 111:4; 145:8 (NIV).

13 John 11:46–53 (NIV).

14 Matthew 14:14 (NIV).

15 Mark 6:31 (ESV).

16 Matthew 20:18–19 (NIV).

17 Matthew 20:30–34 (NIV).

18 Matthew 21:14 (NIV).

19 Matthew 9:35–36 (NIV).

20 Psalm 23:1–3 (NIV).

21 Psalm 23:4–6 (NLT).

22 Psalm 100:3 (NIV).

23 Jonah 4:11 (NIV).

24 Strong's Exhaustive Concordance of the Bible.

25 Keil and Deilitzsch, *Commentaries on the Old Testament, Minor Prophets*, vol. 1, p. 416.

26 Genesis 6:8–9 (NIV).

27 Job 42:10, 12 (NIV).

28 Second Chronicles 20:7; James 2:23 (NIV).

29 Malachi 1:2 (NIV).

30 Numbers 12:6–8 (NIV).

31 Judges 13:5 (NIV).

32 Judges 14:6, 19; 15:14 (NIV).

33 First Kings 19:3–4 (NIV).

34 Matthew 17:3 (NIV).

35 Hebrews 12:6 (NIV).

36 Acts 13:22 (NIV).

37 Luke 7:28 (NIV).

38 Acts 2:41 (NIV).

39 Acts 15:37–39 (NIV); Second Timothy 4:11 (NIV).

40 Philippians 3:12 (NLT).

41 Ephesians 3:8 (NIV).

42 Psalm 103:13–17 CSB

43 Isaiah 54:7–8 (NIV).

44 Isaiah 49:15–16 (NIV).

45 Lamentations 3:21–23 (NIV).

46 Jeremiah 31:20 (NIV).

47 Hosea 11:1, 8 (NIV).

48 Nehemiah 9:17–18 (NIV).

49 Joel 2:13 (NIV).

50 Ecclesiastes 3:11 (NIV).

51 John 3:19 (NASB).

52 Luke 13:3,5 (NIV).

53 Second Peter 3:9 (NIV).

54 John 3:16 (NIV).

55 John 3:17 (NIV).

56 First Timothy 2:3–4 (NIV).

57 First Corinthians 2:9 (NIV).

58 Wikipedia. *Sinners in the Hands ...*

59 Matthew 3:7 (ESV).

60 Larry Dixon, former professor of theology, Columbia Biblical Seminary of Columbia International University.

61 Matthew 8:12; 13:42, 50; Luke 13:28 (ESV).

62 Matthew 13:42, 50 (ESV).

63 Matthew 18:8; 25:41 (NIV).

64 Matthew 3:12; Mark 9:43; Luke 3:17 (ESV).

65 Luke 16:24 (NIV).

66 Matthew 8:12; 22:13; 25:30 (ESV).

67 Jude 13 (NIV).

68 Hebrew 10:31 (ESV).

69 Christian History Institute, *A Prayer Meeting That Lasted 100 Years.*

70 Wikipedia. *Moravian slaves.*

BIBLIOGRAPHY

Adkins, Donna; https://genius.com/The-worship-initiative-glorify-thy-name.

Armstronginstitute.org Jerusalem's temples: the archeological evidence.

Christian History Institute. https://christianhistory institute.org. *A Prayer Meeting That Lasted 100 Years.*

Edwards, William D.; Gabel, Wesley J.; Hosmer, Floyd E. https://dbmz6k5r32451.cloudfront.net/wp-content/uploads/On-the-Physical-Death-of-Jesus-Christ-Jama-1986.pdf.

Geldenhuys, Norval. *Commentary on the Gospel of Luke.* [The New International Commentary on the New Testament] Grand Rapids, MI: Wm. B. Eerdmans Publishing Co., 1951.

Keil, C. F. and F. Delitzsch. *Commentaries on the Old Testament, the Pentateuch.* vol. 1. Grand Rapids, MI: Wm. B. Eerdmans Publishing Co., 1968.

Keil, C.F. and F. Delitzsch, *Commentaries on the Old Testament, Minor Prophets*, vol. 1, Grand Rapids, MI: Wm. B. Eerdmans Publishing Co., 1969.

Kinlaw, Dennis F, 1984. *This Day with the Master, 365 Daily Meditations*, "October 24" Napponee, IN: Francis Asbury Press.

Lane, William. *The Gospel According Mark*. [The New International Commentary on the New Testament]. Wm. B. Eerdmans Publishing Co., Grand Rapids, MI., 1974.

Livingston, David: https://www.goodreads.com/quotes/672075

McConkey, James. *"Revival and the Holy Spirit"*. https://www.path2prayer.com.

Morris, Leon: *The Gospel According to John*. [The New International Commentary on the New Testament] Grand Rapids, MI: Wm. B. Eerdmans Publishing Co., 1971.

Oatman, Johnson, Jr. *"What the Angels Sing"*. Hagerstown, MD: Review and Herald Publishing Association, 1985. https://www.sdahymnal.org.

Paget, Catesby. https://hymnary.org/text/near_so_very_near_to_god

Peterson, John W.: *"In the Image of God"*. © 1957 John W. Peterson Music Company. All rights reserved. Used by permission.

Piper, John. *Let the Nations Be Glad! The Supremacy of God in Missions*. Grand Rapids, MI: Baker Academic, 1972.

Ross, Alexander: *The Epistles of James and John*. [New International Commentary on the New Testament]. Grand Rapids, MI: Wm. B. Eerdmans Publishing Co., 195

Rutherford, Samuel. https://www.azquotes.com/author/12820-Samuel_Rutherford.

Walvoord, John. The Abrahamic Covenant and Premillennialism. https://bible.org>seriespage>12-a

Wikipedia. Covenant (biblical) [https://en.wikipedia.org/wiki/Covenant_(biblical)]

Wikipedia. https://en.m.wikipedia.org. *Moravian slaves.*

Wikipedia. *Sinners in the Hands of an Angry God Great Awakening*

EPILOGUE

Early in my life, I became aware that the Gospel of Christ was completely unknown in many parts of the world. That awareness was intensified when my father resigned as the successful pastor of a thriving church in America—to spend most of the rest of his working life making Christ known in northern Gold Coast (now Ghana), where, at that time, no one had ever heard of Christ. My father's missionary passion was contagious, and I determined to spend my life in the same way. Eventually, the Lord led my wife and me to Papua New Guinea, where, with our two young children, we began living among the twenty-two thousand Duna people, none of whom had heard of Christ. We were motivated by a desire to be used of God in bringing them to saving faith.

One morning, during my quiet time with the Lord, I came in scripture to a text that referred to Christ's followers as his bride. I realized for the first time that my wife and I were being privileged to help prepare Christ's bride for the day when he would take her to himself in a heavenly wedding. Furthermore, from scripture, I knew his bride would be composed of people from every ethnic nation, including some of the Duna people among whom we were living.

That is how, for me, the mission of God became more than the salvation of sinners, important though that is. It had to do with preparing a bride for Jesus. In that awareness, I prayed, "Lord, I want to spend the rest of my life helping to prepare your bride for that wedding day. And if I'm never privileged to do anything more than to shine the bride's shoes in preparation for that wedding, then I will do that with all my heart for the rest of my life." Ever since then, I've been serving joyfully as the bridegroom's shoeshine boy.

Over the years following that eye-opening understanding, I've become aware of other factors that motivate the missionary heart of God. Although my understanding is no doubt incomplete, in this book I have attempted to write what I have learned, in the hope that this enlarged perspective will help ignite in the hearts of others, as it has for me, a desire to engage fully in bringing to completion this global mission of God.

ABOUT THE AUTHOR

It was the ambition of Dennis Cochrane and his wife, Nancy, to spend their lives making the Good News of Christ known to people among whom Christ was completely unknown. That ambition led them to live, with their two young children, among the animistic Duna people of Papua New Guinea. Many Duna eventually put their faith in Christ and were set free from the constant fear of demonic powers that had previously enslaved them.

When, for health reasons, the Cochranes were unable to continue living overseas, the Lord gave them a new ambition: to challenge the Lord's people in America to become involved in bringing to completion the global mission of God. The Lord honored that ambition by giving Dennis the privilege of teaching numerous mission-mobilization classes nationwide—classes titled "Perspectives on the World Christian Movement." Dennis was comforted with the realization that if he couldn't personally take the Good News of Christ to an unreached people group, perhaps the Lord could use him to send others in his place.